10/09

To Tori + Greg,

With affection, thanks
+ friendship. This* would
not have been possible
without Greg's eagle eye
+ great suggestions.

Nancy

* "This" = PP 73-80!

OTHER DUTIES

AS ASSIGNED

Part of the American Council on Education Series on Higher Education
Susan Slesinger, Executive Editor

Other selected titles in the series:

OTHER DUTIES AS ASSIGNED

Presidential Assistants in Higher Education

Edited by Mark P. Curchack

AMERICAN COUNCIL ON EDUCATION
® The Unifying Voice for Higher Education

ROWMAN & LITTLEFIELD EDUCATION

A division of

ROWMAN & LITTLEFIELD PUBLISHERS, INC.

Lanham • New York • Toronto • Plymouth, UK

Published in partnership with the American Council on Education

Published by Rowman & Littlefield Education
A division of Rowman & Littlefield Publishers, Inc.
A wholly owned subsidiary of The Rowman & Littlefield Publishing Group, Inc.
4501 Forbes Boulevard, Suite 200, Lanham, Maryland 20706
http://www.rowmaneducation.com

Estover Road, Plymouth PL6 7PY, United Kingdom

British Library Cataloguing in Publication Information Available

Library of Congress Cataloging-in-Publication Data

Other duties as assigned : presidential assistants in higher education / edited by Mark P. Curchack.
    p. cm. — (American Council on Education series on higher education)
  "Published in partnership with the American Council on Education."
  Includes bibliographical references.
  ISBN 978-1-60709-172-1 (cloth : alk. paper) — ISBN 978-1-60709-174-5 (electronic)
  1. College administrators—United States. 2. Universities and colleges—United States—Employees. 3. Administrative assistants—United States. I. Curchack, Mark P. II. American Council on Education.
  LB2341.O9 2009
  378.1'11—dc22   2009017122

⊚ ™ The paper used in this publication meets the minimum requirements of American National Standard for Information Sciences—Permanence of Paper for Printed Library Materials, ANSI/NISO Z39.48-1992.

Printed in the United States of America

CONTENTS

v

FOREWORD

The Beatles struck a chord with all of us in their song "With a Little Help from My Friends." But the idea is as old as creation—literally. In Genesis, God gives to Adam a "help meet," which is the English translation of a Hebrew phrase meaning, more or less, "an ally alongside." Until comparatively recently when the idea of romantic love became a part, or at least an intention, of marriage, couples came together because both needed someone alongside to help out.

And it's not just couples. There are fewer and fewer lone wolves in the modern world. The complexities of contemporary life require help, teamwork, cooperation, all words implying someone—and often several ones—alongside. This is most surely true of university presidents. There is, I know, an abiding image of the university or college president as a good-natured, wise fellow who came out of the faculty and benignly deals with all problems and all comers on his own. A lovely image, but antediluvian—which means at least fifty years out of date. The university president may be good-natured and wise (I hope I am), but he is as likely to be a woman as a man, may never have been on a faculty, and—all his or her good nature and wisdom notwithstanding—is completely unequipped to deal with *all* problems and *all* comers *all* the time.

It is for this reason that university hierarchies look very much like the hierarchies in private businesses and public bureaucracies. We call it the division of labor. But even so, the labors reserved to the university president are complex, and often detailed, beyond the grasp or control of any one person. Enter, therefore, the presidential assistant.

This person may take many forms. In fact, a good presidential assistant is something of a chameleon or a shape-shifter, able to adapt to changing landscapes and circumstances—those landscapes and circumstances being the needs, and often the moods, of the president. Thus, an assistant may at times look like a secretary (a word that, I am told, is not really tolerated in polite circles any longer), an alter ego, a counselor, a consultant, a scheduler, a meal orderer, a debating partner, someone to trust, and a valet. And I hasten to remind you of the old phrase, "No man is a hero to his valet."

All these qualities, including the lack of heroism, and many others you will find documented with eyewitness testimony in these pages. That is the point, and the pleasure, of this book, and I will say no more about the contents lest I steal the writers' thunder. But I will add a personal note about my own assistant, Helene Interlandi. She has worked *for* and *with* me for a quarter of a century. She has fulfilled all the roles I listed above and many more over the years. But simply, she has been a helpmeet, understanding both what I need and what my position demands and constantly helping me to meet my responsibilities. Without her alongside me, I would have been at sea more often than I care to think.

And like presidential assistants everywhere, she has done all this with much less recognition than any university president routinely gets. I hope I have thanked her often enough; I thank her now. And I hope this book will inspire thanks to, and recognition of, all PAs who have served their presidents as well as Helene has served me.

Stephen Joel Trachtenberg, president emeritus
and University Professor of Public Administration,
The George Washington University

PREFACE

Mark P. Curchack

"Standing somewhere between Count Richelieu and the doorman," was how one presidential assistant put it.[1] When I began my work as a presidential assistant, I noticed that my employee number was 007. This came to symbolize less the lethal nature of the job, but more the air of mystery that surrounds it. This volume is an attempt to demystify this growing profession.

The role of presidential assistant is a recent one in American higher education. So recent, in fact, that in 1987, Pamela Transue, then presidential assistant at the University of Washington, reached (by telephone) twenty-four other presidential assistants all around the country, "all of whom seemed startled and delighted to learn that there might be other struggling subalterns like themselves out there."[2]

Even though the position may be only about forty years old, the numbers of people on American campuses called assistant to the president, executive assistant, chief of staff, or a host of other titles, have mushroomed in the intervening years. A professional association, the National Association of Presidential Assistants in Higher Education (NAPAHE) has followed from this growth, and in some ways may have stimulated it. NAPAHE grew out of the meeting that Pamela Transue was organizing in 1987. By 1993, the annual meeting of about one hundred assistants formally adopted the NAPAHE name and set about incorporating and, thereby, formalizing its status as an organization. NAPAHE established a formal association with the American Council on Education (ACE), and received great assistance from ACE in its formative years. The annual meeting of NAPAHE takes place along with the ACE national convention. NAPAHE has prospered ever since, usually having between four hundred and six hundred dues-paying members.

In 1995, the association decided it would be valuable to conduct a study of "the profession" to gather more empirical data about the considerable variety and essential commonality that was observed at every meeting. This effort was initiated by then–NAPAHE chair Roland Smith (then at Notre Dame, now an associate provost at Rice University). A large survey was sent to over 900 potential respondents, and over 725 were completed; the process was managed by faculty and graduate students at Teachers College of Columbia University. Much of the data referenced in the pages that follow come from that survey.

At about the same time, NAPAHE decided to pursue the creation of a monograph about presidential assistants, supported by the data of the survey and including chapters by PAs about the many dimensions of the job. The initial plan was to have a primary author for each topic, who would share a first draft with a panel of other PAs with similar positions, in order to have a wider perspective on the issue at hand. In most cases this took place, and the reviewers are noted in each chapter along with the author. This volume is the outcome of those efforts.

In the chapters that follow, fifteen present and former PAs discuss the most common components of the role of presidential assistant, as well as general dimensions of the position. Other authors include, in one instance, someone who was a graduate student involved in the survey research, and in a second instance, speechwriters with long associations with PAs. We begin with the two most data-rich chapters. First is a statistical study of the career paths to becoming a PA, written by Belinda Miles, then the associate dean and now the president of Cuyahoga Community College. Her analysis is derived from her doctoral dissertation carried out on the original NAPAHE data set at Teachers College of Columbia University.

Next, Emily Sinsabaugh, then assistant to the president at Edinboro University of Pennsylvania, now vice president for university relations at St. Bonaventure University, looks at the issue of gender in the role of the PA, both theoretically and through the survey data. This had been a perennial topic at NAPAHE meetings, spawned by the easy confusion between executive assistants and administrative assistants. Then, drawing heavily upon discussions at those meetings and on articles published about PAs, Laura

Katrenicz, executive assistant to the president at Luzerne County Community College, analyzes the central qualities of presidential assistants.

We next turn to several of the most common features of the PA role. Marc Schaeffer, chief of staff of William Paterson University of New Jersey, writes about managing the president's office, while Toni Gifford, director of institutional research and former special assistant to the president at Bank Street College of Education, looks at managing the life of the president.

The two chapters that follow look at the linked roles of PAs as fundraisers and as speechwriters. The first is by Marcus Lingenfelter, once executive assistant to the president at Widener University, now vice president for university advancement at Harrisburg University of Science and Technology, and Michael McGreevey, vice president for development at Wells College and former senior advisor to the president, Ithaca College; the second is by Richard P. Haven, professor of communication and interim dean, College of Arts and Communication, University of Wisconsin–Whitewater, and Kevin Boatright, director of communications, Office of Research and Graduate Studies, University of Kansas.

Many PAs, perhaps as many 30 percent, also serve as secretaries to their boards of trustees, and Nancy Kelly, senior advisor to the president and secretary of Hampshire College, explores this common dual role. All university personnel handle complaints from time to time, but a PA is in a special position with regard to the complaint process, as analyzed by Steve Givens, associate vice chancellor and director of university communications (formerly assistant to the chancellor), Washington University of St. Louis. Mark Curchack, associate vice president for planning and assessment, executive director of the president's office, and secretary to the board at Arcadia University, then examines the ways in which PAs can be or become senior administrators, formally or informally.

We return to an exploration of career issues for PAs. Elizabeth Schoenfeld, executive assistant to the president at Western Washington University, looks at those PAs who spend an entire career as a presidential assistant, or at least who retire from such a post. Tony Ross, associate to the president at Wichita State University (now vice president for student affairs, California State University, Los Angeles) then looks at what PAs can do and have done in roles after serving as PAs. Finally, John Cummins, retired associate chancellor and chief of staff to the chancellor, University of California, Berkeley, tells us about "Juggling Jell-O: Other Duties as Assigned," where we get the title of this volume, and very likely the motto PAs might use on an official seal.

The volume concludes with two chapters about presidential assistants that originally appeared as talks given by some very senior PAs at NAPAHE meetings. The first, by NAPAHE cofounder and first convener Pamela Transue, president of Tacoma Community College, explores her idea that a PA is like a courtier in a Renaissance court. Finally, we have the witty version of life as a presidential assistant, as described by another NAPAHE cofounder, the late James Scally.

We are also indebted to President Stephen Joel Trachtenberg, always a friend of NAPAHE, for his most generous foreword to this volume.

NOTES

1. James Scally, then-assistant to the president at the University of Kansas, in an address to the January 18, 1989, meeting of presidential assistants.

2. Pamela Transue, personal communication.

❶

FROM WHENCE THEY CAME: CAREER PATHS TO THE PRESIDENTIAL ASSISTANT POSITION

Belinda Miles

Those who aspire to be presidential assistants, or those interested in identifying, targeting, or grooming candidates for those positions may wonder from where these versatile administrators hail. What types of jobs lead to this "high-level staff officer" role (Fisher, 1985) that involves considerable decision making, judgment, and confidentiality along with frequent interaction with a wide range of leaders and other individuals in the higher education sector (Carlson, 1991)? What types of positions comprise the pathways to this multifaceted presidential support role? Discovering patterns among the prior roles held by presidental assistants (PAs) will increase our understanding about the divergent routes that may be taken or sources that might be tapped to fill this complex position.

Therefore, this chapter discusses career paths that lead to PA positions in higher education. Based on data from the national study of PAs described in the preface, I analyze the varied prior positions that commonly precede that of PA. The chapter also includes a brief overview of relevant career path concepts as well as a discussion of methods used in this research. In addition, I present a discussion of how various demographic characteristics influence career paths to the PA role. The chapter concludes with a discussion of how PA career path analysis can inform both career and institutional planning in higher education administration.

THE NATURE OF THE STUDY DATA

The data used to generate the information featured in this report were derived from a national survey of PAs in higher education conducted by a team of researchers at Columbia University Teachers College, as described in the preface to this book.

The assumptions and limitations of these data raise some cautions about the use and interpretation of the study results. First, this study assumed that PA functions are similar in most aspects, given the general uniformity seen in higher education administrative position classifications (Higher Education Directory, 1998). The research centered on examination of position titles only and did not probe for information about the range of duties or experiences within the titles. It is likely, however, that positions with the same title may encompass a wide range of duties that vary across higher education institutions. Furthermore, since data used in this study were collected in the spring of 1996, we cannot control for any changes in demographic profile, or even career paths that might have transpired. Finally, survey respondents who did not complete data regarding their career histories or submit relevant portions of their vitae could not be identified for follow-up, due to efforts to maintain participants' anonymity. Thus, nonrespondents might have had different career paths than did respondents. However, the high yield on this census survey mitigates this limitation.

CAREER PATH CONCEPT AND METHODOLOGIES

This section presents an overview of career path concepts and methodologies used in this study, which provides background to aid in the understanding of its results.

Career Path Concepts

Spilerman's (1977) notion of viewing career paths backward from a particular position is a central underpinning of this study. Twombly's (1985) idea of determining career paths by analyzing previous positions held in common by specified proportions of subjects was also employed. The technique developed by Moore et al. (1983) and Salimbene (1982) for determining variations of the principal or normative career path by identifying key positions in a principal career path that were skipped was also incorporated in this research.

Methodology

This study used titles listed in the 1998 Higher Education Directory (1998) and those reported in the career history section of the survey or vitae provided by study participants (table 1.1) to determine career paths. Three types of career paths to the PA position were discerned for analysis in this study: the principal career path (PCP), principal career path variations (PCP variations), and the career path comprehensive (CPC). The PCP was established by selecting the single career path that had the highest percentage of individuals who held a first prior position in common and other prior positions along the same path. In the event of a tie, selecting the career path that had the highest percentage of individuals who held a second prior position in common identified the principal career path. This step was repeated for each prior position as needed, as ties occurred.

Variations of the PCP were determined by analyzing the number of positions along the PCP that were omitted on the path to the PA role. Each position in the PCP was assigned a numerical value: 3rd prior position = 1, 2nd prior position = 10, and 1st prior position = 100. An analytical formula in which the sum of these values is equal to the PCP to the PA position was used to determine the existence of alternate career paths to the PA position. Thus, 1 (3rd prior position) + 10 (2nd prior position) + 100 (1st prior position) = 111. Additional details of how the numerical codes and analytical formula were devised and applied are found elsewhere in the literature (Miles, 2000).

The CPC depicts all positions immediately prior to the PA post held by at least 10 percent of the study population. Beyond these positions, the

Table 1.1.   Position Titles Used in This Study

Presidential Assistant
President/Chief Executive Officer/Campus Executive
Vice President (academic)
Vice President (nonacademic)
Deans/Director (academic)
Deans/Director (nonacademic)
Associate/Assistant/Professional Staff
Department Chair
Faculty Positions
Higher Education Secretarial/Clerical
Outside Higher Education Professional
Outside Higher Education Specialist
Outside Higher Education Teacher
Outside Higher Education Secretarial/Clerical
Outside Higher Education Other

CPC also denotes positions held second prior to the PA post by at least 5 percent of those who share the most common positions held immediately prior to the PA job. For a more in-depth description of this method, see Miles (2000).

Results

Principal Career Path   This study identified a PCP to the position of college PA consisting of four positions, that of outside higher education secretarial/clerical, then higher education secretarial/clerical, then associate director/assistant director/professional staff, and, finally, presidential assistant. The PCP explained the career path experience of .9 percent ($n = 7$) of the study population. Figure 1.1 depicts an image of the principal career path to the PA position.

PCP Variations   The study also identified seven variations of the PCP as alternate paths to the PA role. Three (12.7 percent) of these variations involved the omission of one PCP position. Three (46.5 percent) of the variations involved omission of two PCP positions. The final variation included no PCP positions (39.8 percent). Hence, most respondents (60.1 percent) held at least one position on the PCP. Table 1.2 depicts the distribution of study participants who traveled the PCP and PCP variations en route to the PA post.

Presidential assistant
(n=738)

□

Associate director/
Assistant director/
Professional staff
(n=166, 22.5%)

□

Higher education
secretary/clerical
(n=27, 3.6%)

□

Outside higher education
secretary/clerical
(n=4, .5%)

Figure 1.1. Principal Career Path to the PA Position

PCP, PCP Variations, and Related Characteristics   Pearson's correlations were used to provide further substance and definition to the PCP and its variations. Nine categories of variables were tested against the PCP, the PCP variations, and the non-PCP experiences to determine whether statistically significant relationships exist: gender, race, education level, institutional status, Carnegie classification, job level, institutional size, salary, and key jobs.

The PCP was positively correlated with holding less than a bachelor's degree ($p < .05$), holding only a professional degree ($p < .01$), and being in a position classified as professional level ($p < .01$). The PCP was negatively correlated with being in a senior management position ($p < .01$).

The PCP variations, which indicated the experience of nearly 60 percent of the study population, were positively correlated with being female ($p < .01$), not holding a doctorate ($p < .01$), holding less than a bachelor's degree ($p < .05$), being in a position classified as either middle management ($p < .05$) or professional ($p < .01$), and earning a salary of less than $40,000 per year ($p < .01$). The PCP variations were negatively correlated with being

Table 1.2.   Career Path Variations

		N	%
Perfect match		7	0.95
Missing 1 Position			
Minus outside higher education secretarial/clerical		41	5.56
Minus associate director/assistant director/ professional staff		49	6.64
Minus higher education secretarial/clerical		4	0.54
	Subtotal	94	12.74
Missing 2 Positions			
Minus higher education secretarial/ clerical and outside higher education secretarial/clerical		231	31.30
Minus associate director/assistant director/professional staff and outside higher education secretarial/clerical		74	10.03
Minus associate director/assistant director/professional staff and higher education secretarial/clerical		38	5.15
	Subtotal	343	46.48
Missing 3 Positions			
Minus associate director/assistant director/professional staff, higher education secretarial/clerical, and outside higher education secretarial/clerical		294	39.84
	Total	738	100.0

male ($p < .01$), holding a doctorate ($p < .01$), working at a religiously affiliated institution ($p < .01$), holding a middle senior position ($p < .01$), and
earning a salary of more than \$60,000 per year ($p < .01$). PCP variations
were also negatively correlated with holding second prior positions as either
K–12 teachers ($p < .05$) or faculty ($p < .01$).

The PCP variation that excluded all PCP positions prior to the PA role
and representing the experiences of close to 40 percent of the study population was positively correlated with being male ($p < .01$), holding a doctorate
($p < .01$), working at a religiously affiliated institution ($p < .01$), being in a
senior management position ($p < .01$), and earning a salary of more than
\$60,000 per year ($p < .01$). This variation was also positively correlated with
holding second prior positions as either K–12 teachers ($p < .05$) or faculty
($p < .01$). Further, this variation was negatively correlated with being female ($p < .01$), with holding a bachelor's degree ($p < .05$) or less ($p < .01$),
or no doctorate ($p < .01$). Finally, this alternate path was also negatively
correlated with being in middle management ($p < .05$) or professional ($p <
.01$) positions and earning a salary of less than \$40,000 per year ($p < .01$).

The PCP and its variations may be construed as three different types of
career paths. The PCP includes all positions identified using the designated
PCP methodology. The PCP variations involving at least one but not all of
the PCP positions may be labeled as PCP variations. The final category, the
PCP variation that did not include any PCP positions prior to the PA role,
may be regarded as a non-PCP. Using this typology, study data revealed
that these three types of career paths were negatively correlated with each
other ($p < .05$). Table 1.3 highlights these differences.

Career Path Comprehensive

The CPC comprises the PCP and several other career paths ($n = 13$)
traversed en route to the PA post. It depicts all positions immediately prior

Table 1.3. Differences in PCP, PCP Variations, and Non-PCP Experiences

Career Path Type	Correlated with This Career Path Type	Direction of Correlation and Significance Level
PCP	PCP Variations	Negative ($p < .01$)
	Non-PCP Experiences	Negative ($p < .05$)
PCP Variations	PCP	Negative ($p < .01$)
	Non-PCP Experiences	Negative ($p < .01$)
Non-PCP Experiences	PCP	Negative ($p < .05$)
	PCP Variations	Negative ($p < .01$)

to the PA post held by at least 10 percent of the study population. The CPC also shows second prior positions held by at least 5 percent of those first prior positions filled at the 10 percent or more level. However, while second prior positions were calculated based on percentages of the first prior positions they preceded, they are reported as percentages of the entire study population (n = 738). The CPC omits third prior positions because the numbers of PAs in such positions were so small that they added neither meaning nor distinction to the career path typologies portrayed. The CPC is unique in that it highlights the PCP as the career line that begins with the largest single group of individuals in a position immediately prior to the PA role alongside other popular paths to the post.

The CPC shows that the three main portals to the PA post are the associate director/assistant director/professional staff, nonacademic dean or director, and higher education secretarial/clerical positions. These three positions and the thirteen paths from which they ascended explained the experience of 54.9 percent of the 738 PAs studied.

DISCUSSION

Principal Career Path

The PCP failed to explain the career path experience of nearly all PAs (99.1 percent) who participated in this study. This occurred partly because the PCP is based on the largest single group of individuals who hold a first prior career position in common. While the number identified may represent the largest single group of individuals in a single first prior position, it automatically excludes the sum of all other remaining groups of individuals in other commonly held positions. This practice severely limits the ability of the PCP to provide a more inclusive view of the roads taken to the PA post. This problem is exacerbated by continuing the process of recognizing only the largest single groups of individuals who hold other preceding positions in common because the numbers of individuals who share positions in common decreases as progressively earlier stages on career lines are reached.

Further, the PCP is flawed in its suggestion that only positions identified on a single career line can explain how to reach the PA post. The notion of defining a PCP based on a single career line ignores other positions held by substantial numbers of individuals in the study group that might matter as viable forerunners to the PA role. Obscuring these other PA position antecedents supports the notion of "one best model" but simultaneously prevents enhanced understanding that a more complex analysis otherwise produces.

The PCP seemed most useful for its role in distinguishing the position of associate director/assistant director/professional staff as a frequent precursor to the PA role. More than 22 percent (22.5 percent) of the PAs in this analysis held this post.

PCP Variations

The PCP variations provided a fuller picture of the career path experiences prior to obtaining the PA role than did the actual PCP. The variations revealed that, contrary to occasional perceptions of the PA position as somehow secretarial in nature (Ross & Green, 1990), 71.1 percent of the study population reached the PA post via paths that did not include such experience. Like the PCP, the PCP variation analysis also provided evidence that the associate director/assistant director/professional staff role is key in the path to the PA position. A total of 38.3 percent of study participants held these kinds of posts. Still, despite the increased description of PA pathways facilitated by analyzing various combinations of the PCP, nearly 40 percent (39.8 percent) reached the post without any combination of PCP positions.

The limitations of the PCP and its variations in describing the PA role are significant because they point to a need for more inclusive ways to document career development in higher education administrative careers. The PCP analysis alone was nearly devoid of value. The PCP analysis juxtaposed with the PCP variation analysis achieved a more thorough analysis of the prior employment experiences of an appreciable portion of the PAs in this study, but only a portion.

The negative correlation among the PCP, PCP variations, and non-PCP indicates that the differences in how the PA post was reached were not subtle or slight. Put another way, distinct features characterize the diverse paths that lead to the PA job and these raise both questions and concerns. Are women less successful at negotiating better salaries for the PA roles they obtain? It may be that men bring a different set of skills and background to the post that qualifies them for better-paying and higher-level PA positions. Is women's lack of more advanced credentials a hindrance to reaching more powerful types of PA jobs? Do men feel more comfortable leaving the presumably safe domains of K–12 teaching and faculty jobs for administrative careers in the academy? Perhaps, conversely, women are more willing to remain in teaching jobs because such jobs offer more security and flexibility than the PA role might. Additionally, women may be less willing to leave these types of jobs to take on PA roles that may not seem stable or powerful. This situation could result in a smaller pool of highly educated women who opt for PA posts.

Career Path Comprehensive

The CPC provided a broader and more inclusive view of the paths to the PA job than either the PCP analysis or the PCP subgroup analysis. It clearly described three major portals to the PA role as well as many antecedents to these portals. The CPC included more than half (54.9 percent) of the study participants in its simple depiction of roads traveled to the PA job. The CPC not only enables individuals with disparate career backgrounds to "find" themselves on the road to becoming a PA but also allows them to easily compare their track to the post with paths taken by others.

PAs who came from outside higher education filled each of the three first prior CPC positions. For example, each was filled, in part, with people who held jobs previously such as office manager, project director, or human resource manager or with workers previously employed as outside higher education specialists in positions such as attorney, accountant, or editor. Teachers from the K–12 arena filled the nonacademic dean or director posts as well. The higher education secretarial/clerical jobs drew from the outside higher education secretarial/clerical pool of workers.

Workers with employment experience within higher education also filled each of the three primary precursor positions. Faculty members found their way into either the associate director/assistant director/professional staff and nonacademic dean or director roles. Nonacademic deans or directors went to associate director/assistant director/professional staff roles, and vice versa. Associate director/assistant director/professional staff even moved into higher education secretarial/clerical work on occasion.

Thus, the three most popular roles that preceded the PA position showed that those already employed within higher education most often filled the PA position. However, the experiences prior to these three roles were more diverse, revealing access both for those within and outside of academe. This revealed some flexibility in hiring practices of organizations willing to take the risk of bringing "outsiders" into the academic environment. This finding also suggests that presidents are looking not only for specific jobs that may appear to be "stair steps" to the PA role. Rather, they more likely prefer an accumulation of skills or a match of styles that may be found in places other than academe.

Finally, the CPC confirms that the associate director/assistant director/ professional staff job factors heavily on the path to the PA position. The position was a direct forerunner to the PA job and was also situated prior to other key immediate PA forerunners. Either way, it was a prevalent post on the path to becoming a PA.

As a composite of key positions held prior to the PA role, the CPC provides an inclusive view of many diverse and divergent paths to the PA job. This network of passageways simultaneously highlights and subordinates the PCP as a path to the PA post. Entrance to key higher education administrative jobs leading to the PA post occurs at various levels and from various places. Professional office workers and other specially trained individuals from outside academe can launch into professional or support staff roles that get them noticed and arm them with skills needed for eventual upward mobility to the PA post.

This overview reveals the many layers and textures involved in advancing to the PA post. The analysis also helps to assess how similar or dissimilar access to this post is for various groups of workers. CPC findings also disclose higher education administrative posts that did not show up on the various career lines. For example, the absence of presidents on the CPC suggests that these higher education leaders do not "step back" into PA posts. The PA post also does not draw significantly from the ranks of either academic or nonacademic vice presidents. It is likely that academic vice presidents are on a different career path, perhaps to the presidency, at this stage of their careers. Nonacademic vice presidents may be at what is considered the top of the career line for their field. Department chairs also do not show up on the CPC. Similar to academic vice presidents, it is likely that these administrators have career goals that do not include obtaining the PA job.

Variables That Affect Paths

Considerable differentiation exists with regard to how the PA position is obtained.

Gender   Women differ from men in how they reach the PA function. Despite their high numbers in the position, variables associated with the PCP variations indicate that females are clustered in less formidable middle-management or professional-level PA jobs than are males.

These results raise both a sense of hope and alarm. If the PA position serves as a potential springboard for women to launch into more professional careers, this is the good news. The not-so-good news is that, despite the nearly three-to-one ratio of women to men in the field, men are prospering more in the field.

Educational background   Level of education matters in becoming a PA and in the type of PA position obtained. Variables associated with non-PCP experiences reveal the potency of doctoral degrees in leading to higher-level-type PA jobs than posts obtained by those who lack the credential. Variables correlated with the PCP and its variations show that possession of less than a bachelor's degree relegates individuals in this category to mostly middle-management-type PA positions. This may be a factor of too little training and experience in the more global and analytical thinking that presumably comes with advanced levels of education. It could also be attributed to the inability of PAs to meet minimal educational standards set by institutions for hiring staff into upper administrative ranks.

Education-related findings from this study document the rewards associated with the attainment of advanced education but also highlight discrepancies between the education "haves" and "have nots." Earned graduate degrees seem to be a key link to better types of PA jobs. Regrettably, data from this study indicate that women lag far behind men with regard to educational credentials. Supplemental data analyses of the PAs in this study show that one-fifth (20.9 percent) of the female PAs studied held less than a bachelor's degree ($p < .01$). No male PAs were in this category ($p < .01$). About one-fourth of the women in the study (25.9 percent) held only a bachelor's degree ($p < .01$) compared with only 6.9 percent of men in this category ($p < .01$). The gap between male and female PAs who hold master's degrees was less severe: 29.6 percent for men and 24 percent for women. However, men with professional degrees, doctorates, or some doctoral studies (63.5 percent) outnumbered women (29.2 percent) by over two to one in this category. Further, being male was positively correlated with holding doctorates ($p < .01$) or professional degrees ($p < .05$) but being female was not ($p < .05$).

The doctorate seemed to benefit both male and female PAs with the credential. Both men and women with doctorates were found in PA jobs that paid $60,000 or more ($p < .01$). Women accessed such jobs from roles such as academic dean or director ($p < .01$). Men also accessed them from those roles ($p < .01$) as well as from the associate director/assistant director/professional staff position ($p < .01$). Pearson's correlation analyses confirmed the statistical significance of these findings as indicated. Hence, while education is a major factor that contributes to advanced standing in the PA occupation, women are more often excluded from widespread enjoyment of this benefit since they trail men considerably in education. The results clearly support prior studies regarding the superiority of holding a doctoral degree versus not having one when pursuing higher education administrative careers (Dorich, 1991; Lunsford, 1984; Moore, 1985; Moore & Twombly, 1990; Ostroth, Efird, & Lerman, 1984).

Implications for Practice

The various inequities discussed in this chapter about paths to PA roles in higher education point to a need for change for the profession. Policymakers in colleges and universities should examine their operations to identify existing pay and status inequities that might be occurring among PAs on their campuses based on gender lines. While it is possible that differential pay or job status might occur based on institutional need, policymakers and hiring officers should take special care to ensure that such decisions are not based on gender alone.

Further, college and university officials and administrators should be supportive and sensitive regarding PAs who are pursuing advanced degrees. They should understand that those with advanced degrees could contribute more to their operations in senior-level capacities. They should also recognize that supporting women as they pursue advanced education would help make these employees more valuable resources for their institutions. Support could include such ideas as providing flexible work schedules or creative use of earned compensatory time.

When making employment decisions about PAs, college and university officials and administrators should recognize that the range of prior positions that are appropriate precursors to the post is considerable. Qualified applicants need not be limited to those found within higher education institutions. Rather, emphasis should be placed on the actual skills and abilities needed for the job, which could have been developed in positions outside higher education.

Aspiring PAs should be aware of how the pursuit and attainment of advanced education and employment choices can influence their careers as PAs. For example, those with doctoral degrees are likely to land better-paying and higher-status PA positions. In addition, given the dynamic nature of the PA role, which changes to meet presidential needs, even those with terminal degrees should actively consider lifelong learning opportunities that could enhance their ability to meet the demands of their PA roles.

Finally, professional development staff and graduate school admissions professionals should actively promote the PA profession and educational opportunities that could lead to the post. The PA position seems to be a growing administrative function in the higher education arena. Just over 1,900 existed in 1996 when data for this project were collected. It is plausible that several hundred more such roles exist currently to meet institutional needs and demands for the function. Some presidential suites now employ two or more PAs to meet the specialized needs that exist.

CONCLUSION

This study of PA career paths revealed that there is no "one best way" to reach the post. Neither the identified PCP nor its variations fully depicted the prior employment experiences of PAs. The CPC provided a better understanding about paths taken to the post, but still only just for over half the sample. The diverse ways of getting to the PA role reveal the complexity associated with career path documentation of this role. The role is not likely one that individuals planned to obtain. Rather, various sets of educational and employment experiences seem to have placed individuals in settings that armed them with the skills and abilities to qualify for a dynamic role that is idiosyncratically configured for each president. Personal demographics and educational backgrounds also influenced the paths in important ways.

Findings from this career path study have broad significance. They effectively reveal the overall accessibility of the PA role. However, they also highlight important gender gaps and educational inequalities that characterize experiences that effect routes to the post.

REFERENCES AND FURTHER READING

Carlson, N. L. (1991). Professional roles and functions of presidential assistants in contemporary higher education. Peabody College for Teachers of Vanderbilt University. Ann Arbor, MI.: UMI Dissertation Abstracts No. 9215372.

Dorich, D. (1991). The making of a president. *Currents, 17*(4), 6–11.

Fisher, J. L. (1985). Presidential assistants: An unsung resource. *AGB Reports, 27*(6), 33–36.

Higher Education Directory. (1998). [Online]. www.hepinc.com/highereddir3.htm.

Kauffman, J. F. (1990). Administration then and now. In *Administrative Careers and the Marketplace: New Directions for Higher Education #72, 18*(4), 99–107.

Kerlinger, F. N. (1986). *Foundations of behavioral research.* Orlando, FL: Harcourt Brace.

Lunsford, L. (1984). Chief student affairs officer: The ladder to the top. *NASPA Journal, 22*(1), 48–56.

Miles, B. S. (2000). Career paths of presidential assistants in higher education. Doctoral dissertation, Columbia University.

Moore, K. M. (1985). *Administrator mobility: Crossing the boundary between two-year and four-year colleges and universities.* University Park: Pennsylvania State University, Center for the Study of Higher Education.

Moore, K. M. (1995). Universitas. *Review of Higher Education, 18*(4), 467–482.

Moore, K. M., Salimbene, A., Marlier, J., & Bragg, S. (1983). The structure of presidents' and deans' careers. *Journal of Higher Education, 5*, 501–515.

Moore, K. M., & Twombly, S. B. (1990). Toward the year 2000. In *Administrative Careers and the Marketplace: New Directions for Higher Education #72, 18*(4), 109–113.

Ostroth, D. D., Efird, F. D., & Lerman, L. S. (1984). Career patterns of chief student affairs officers. *Journal of College Student Personnel, 25*(5), 443–447.

Pollick, A. M. (1995). Survey sense. *Currents, 21*, 50–54.

Rea, L. M., & Parker, R. A. (1997). *Designing and conducting survey research: A comprehensive guide*. San Francisco: Jossey-Bass.

Ross, M., & Green, M. F. (1990). The rules of the game: The unwritten code of career mobility. In *Administrative Careers and the Marketplace: New Directions for Higher Education #72, 18*(4), 67–77.

Salimbene, A. (1982). Pathways to the presidency: An examination of the careers of current college and university chief executives. Doctoral dissertation, Pennsylvania State University.

Spilerman, S. (1977). Careers, labor market structure, and socio-economic achievement. *American Journal of Sociology, 83*(3), 551–593.

Twombly, S. B. (1985). *The structure of careers of top-level two-year college administrators: An internal labor market approach*. Doctoral dissertation, Pennsylvania State University.

Uehling, B. S. (1981). Building a presidential team. In *Academic Leaders as Managers: New Directions for Higher Education #36, 9*(4), 19–31.

Vaughan, G. B. (1982). Burnout: Threat to presidential effectiveness. *Community and Junior College Journal, 52*(5), 10–13.

2

THE ROLE OF GENDER IN THE PROFESSION OF PRESIDENTIAL ASSISTANT

Emily Sinsabaugh[1]

A review of the ramifications of gender in the profession of the presidential assistant poses some interesting and challenging questions. Some questions are basic, with straightforward answers: Do more women or men serve as presidential assistants (PAs)? Is there a relationship between salary and gender? Other questions are derived from the idiosyncratic nature of the position, with more complicated answers: Are presidential assistants viewed as administrative leaders at their institutions and, if so, are male PAs more likely to be so viewed than their female counterparts? Are men more likely than women to have line responsibilities in their roles as PAs? The real complexity in studying these—and indeed nearly any—questions about presidential assistants is highlighted by Ross and Green (1990), who suggest that job titles are not necessarily indications of roles and responsibilities. *"Assistant to the president* can be a secretarial position or a high-level professional with line responsibility for certain operational areas"* (p. 73). The survey conducted by the National Association of Presidential Assistants in Higher Education (NAPAHE) provides insights into these questions and others, while also being to some degree consistent with the literature on gender and mobility in higher education administration in the United States.

BACKGROUND: GENDER AND HIGHER EDUCATION ADMINISTRATION

Much of the literature on administrative careers and mobility in higher education is presented from the perspective of career paths that lead to positions of perceived power and influence and the extent to which gender plays a role in individuals' opportunities for success. In many respects, discussions from this perspective are not particularly relevant to the position of PA, first because the role is not one that is typically or, at least, explicitly included in studies of higher education administration and, second, because the role is not one that is typically "aspired to." Therefore, the review of literature is applicable to the extent that similarities can be drawn to positions of comparative stature and influence within higher education organizations as well as to the administrative environment in higher education as a whole.

Relative themes that emerge in the literature relate to the effects of perceptual biases, hiring and promotion trends and practices, and ongoing concerns. With regard to perceptions, Konrad and Pfeffer (1991) suggest, "Jobs and occupations come to be seen as typical and more appropriate for men or for women and for whites and minorities" (p. 144). Career advancement for higher education administrators occurs most frequently via intrainstitutional promotions and position changes (Moore, 1983, in Sagaria, 1988). Despite the significant increase of the presence of women in higher education administration, the increase in numbers may not tell the entire story with regard to mobility or ability to advance to positions of influence and power (perceived or otherwise).

Organizational patterns and history can inadvertently assign expectations upon particular jobs or positions as they relate to gender. Bielby and Baron (1986) posit, "Once established, sex labels of job titles acquire tremendous inertia, even when similar work is done by the opposite sex elsewhere in the same establishment or in other settings" (p. 787). Konrad and Pfeffer (1991) report consistency in administrative hiring of women for positions that were previously held by women. "This finding suggests that positions in specific organizations develop gender and ethnic typifications as a result of their local histories of incumbents in the jobs" (p. 153). According to the National Education Association, the number of male administrators in higher education increased by 10 percent in the three decades that followed the implementation of Title IX legislation, while female administrators increased by nearly 150 percent (Opp & Gosetti, 2000). Notwithstanding, Johnsrud and Heck (1994) suggest that considerations of placement, opportunity, and status continue to favor men. A 1997 College and University Professional Association (CUPA) survey revealed that salaries for men exceeded those of women in nearly all of fifty-three selected higher education administrative positions. This finding was consistent at doctoral, comprehensive, baccalaureate and two-year institutions (as cited in Vanderslice and Litsch, 1998).

While, as suggested previously, higher education administrators are more likely to achieve career advancement via internal promotions and position changes, opportunities for women in this regard may be enhanced at institutions where women hold senior leadership positions. A senior management team that reflects a disproportionate number of men can affect hiring decisions as related to gender because of the human propensity to reproduce one's self. Kanter (in Johnsrud and Heck, 1994) tags this behavior *homosocial reproduction*. "Decision makers match persons to jobs but their decisions are a function of social relations as well as of the policy and practice regarding promotion" (Johnsrud, 1991, p. 126). Konrad and Pfeffer (1991) echo these findings: "Organizations in which many women or minorities are currently employed are most likely to place women and minorities in vacant positions" (p. 152). They attribute this finding, in part, to internal promotions.

Enhanced levels of attainment for women continue to be an elusive goal, even in the face of regulations such as affirmative action and Title IX that have undoubtedly influenced the advancement of women in higher education and the move toward the creation of a critical mass both among faculty and administrative ranks. A review of trends in presidential hiring in the United States can serve as a barometer in this regard. According to Ross and Green (2000), "The proportion of women presidents doubled, from 9.5 percent in 1986 to 19.3 percent in 1998. Despite increases at every type of college and university, women still accounted for less than one-fifth of all college presidents" (p. 9). Between 1991 and 1997, white female administrators experienced the largest proportional increase in representation among higher education administration ranks while female administrators of color remained underrepresented proportionally except in minority-serving institutions (Opp & Gosetti, 2000). "Even in institutions where they constitute a substantial proportion of the whole, women faculty and administrators often perceive themselves as being closer to the periphery than to the center of activity—and for women from minority groups, the sense of isolation is even more pronounced" (Knight Higher Education Collaborative, 2001, p. 1). Women are said to be more prevalent in clerical or administrative/staff support positions that are less central to an institution's primary mission, which may affect their range of opportunities for advancement. According to Johnsrud (1991), "At the same time, men are predominant at high levels. Prior location [position held] may serve men as a resource whereas it acts as a vulnerability for women" (p. 130). In a study of hiring and promotion activities between 1969 and 1980, the years during which both affirmative action and Title IX were introduced, Sagaria (1988) concludes that the practice and proliferation of internal promotions of women could serve to create the perception of equal opportunity when, in fact, internal promotions of "known entities" could be a hiring practice that serves to avoid external candidates (women) who are unknown and, thus, potentially disruptive or otherwise undesirable.

As we review the data on PAs related to gender, we are well advised to consider the environment of higher education administration as a whole as depicted in this brief review of literature. The disparities that exist within the presidential assistant profession are, to some extent, consistent with the disparities presented in the literature. Nevertheless, an examination of the data as it relates to this emerging profession is both instructive and thought-provoking.

PRESIDENTIAL ASSISTANTS AND GENDER

Presidential assistants in higher education have been known to lament the gender-related connotations that are often associated with their titles. Those who hold the traditional titles "assistant to the president," "special assistant to the president," or "executive assistant to the president" in particular, have faced some awkward, challenging, or even demeaning situations because of some common associations often made with any person who serves in the role of "assistant." Concerns emerge most often, however, when these associations appear to be based upon assumptions that are linked to a person's gender rather than the person's title or role. One male PA tells of an instance when his president, a woman, was seated at the desk of the office secretary in her absence. The PA happened to be standing next to the secretary's desk at which the president was seated when a guest arrived in the office. Without pause, the guest addressed the PA as president, obviously reflecting the assumption that the male in the office would be serving in the role of president. Correcting this erroneous assumption made for an awkward introduction of the "real" president. Another male PA had ongoing experiences of campus personnel or visitors referring to him in interactions as "her" or "she." Female colleagues repeatedly report experiences where they are referred to as the president's "secretary" or are asked to attend to tasks such as note taking or copying during meetings, or coffee making between meetings—tasks that they are certain would not be expected of them if they were a man in the role of PA. These anecdotal experiences indicate that gender plays a part in the perceptions of the role of the presidential assistant. The data from the NAPAHE survey reveal even more significant differences among the experiences of men and women who serve as PAs in higher education.

Nearly 69 percent of the PAs who responded to the survey were women, reflecting the possibility that the role of presidential assistant is one that has become known as a "woman's role." While slightly more men than women indicated they were the first person of their gender to fill the role of presidential assistant at their institution, the clear majority of both genders indicate they were not the first person of their gender to hold the position. The data do not tell us, however, whether these individuals were the only person of their gender to have held the position at their institution. Although women clearly outnumber men in the profession, these data suggest that, to some degree, the role of PA may not be among those that are characteristically subject to gender typification as described by Konrad and Pfeffer (1991). It is likely that the gender of the PA has more to do with the preference of the president and his or her working style and expectations for the position.

In this context, it is interesting to compare gender to a respondent's institutional type. Nearly 60 percent of the male respondents worked at Master's I and II, Doctoral I and II, and Research I and II institutions compared to 43 percent of women. Women, conversely, had their highest aggregate concentration, nearly 60 percent, in Baccalaureate Liberal Arts I and II and Associate of Arts colleges. Degree attainment could explain the disproportionate number of men at the doctorate and research institutions. Of the total sample, 43 percent of the men had earned doctoral degrees while only 18.6 percent of the women respondents had done so.

Salary comparisons are frequently used as indications of equity among institutions and professions. The 1997–1998 CUPA administrative salary survey cited previously indicated that male PAs made more money than their female counterparts in each of the four institutional classifications (Doctoral, Comprehensive, Baccalaureate, Two-Year). The survey of PAs reveals more of the same, with the largest number of female respondents (60 percent) earning less than $50,000 annually and the largest number of male respondents (60 percent) earning more than $60,000. Of those men earning more than $60,000, 41 percent earned more than $70,000 compared to 14 percent of women reporting the same annual salary. As reported in the previous paragraph, more male than female PAs are employed at Masters I and II, Doctoral I and II, and Research I and II institutions; therefore, one might have predicted this outcome in view of the relationship between salary rates and institutional category.

Next to salary, perhaps the next most frequently cited indicator of status and influence within an institution is whether, and the degree to which, line responsibilities are assigned to the role of the presidential assistant. In our survey, 10 percent more men than women reported having line responsibilities. In addition to serving as a measure of the power and influence of the position within individual institutions, responsibility for institutional operations is regarded as a critical predictor of future career growth options and opportunities. This may suggest that more men than women in the profession are better positioned for career advancement because, as articulated by Johnsrud (1991), having line responsibilities is an occupational "resource." It is appropriate to note here that anecdotal reports from presidential assistants suggest that, in many cases, the PA has no line authority by design so as to enable the position to function at the institution-wide level with no need or impetus to advocate for one division or operation. In this way, the role of the PA can be viewed as impartial or unbiased, which could be a central function of the role and position. Further, it must be noted that the assignment of line responsibilities may be a function of the skills and experiences that a PA brings to the position.

Some of the characteristics of presidential assistants reveal no substantial differences between men and women. There appears to be no significant difference between men and women and the length of service in the position. Interestingly, the majority (74.1 percent for women and 76.2 percent for men) reported being in their positions for less than eight years. This could be related to the tenure of academic presidents in the United States, which, as reported by Ross and Green (2000), averaged 6.9 years in 1998. Less than 10 percent of both male and female respondents had been in their positions for more than fifteen years. Both genders reported nearly equal experiences with mentors, as slightly more than 60 percent of men and women reported participating in a mentoring experience.

In summary, men and women who serve institutions of higher education in the United States in the role of the PA appear to have divergent experiences, as do men and women throughout the realm of higher education administration. It could be surmised that the peculiar nature of the position characteristically calls for such divergence; thus, it would be difficult, if not irresponsible, to draw conclusions about the profession solely by comparing the data on PAs to that collected for other positions of similar stature that have more definitive or standardized roles in higher education. When considering matters of salary and line responsibility alone, however, the data do suggest that more men than women serve in presidential assistant roles that could be characterized as having more influence and higher levels of responsibility. Nevertheless, the sheer number of women in the profession compared to men suggests that the profession is one that is providing opportunities for women in higher education administration. As a relatively new position in higher education administration, it may be too early to know whether these opportunities will result in desired career mobility for the women in the role, or, for that matter, the men.

NOTE

1. With assistance from Honey Bedell, associate director for board services/ executive director, EICCD Foundation, former assistant to the chancellor, Eastern Iowa Community College District; Cindy Heilberger, executive assistant to the president, Pace University; Jeff Johnson, former assistant to the president, University of Puget Sound.

REFERENCES

Bielby, W., & Baron, J. N. (1986). Men and women at work: Sex segregation and statistical discrimination. *American Journal of Sociology, 91,* 759–799.

Johnsrud, L. K. (1991). Administrative promotion: The power of gender. *Journal of Higher Education, 62*(2), 119–149.

Johnsrud, L. K., & Heck, R. H. (1994). Administrative promotion within a university. *Journal of Higher Education, 65*(1), 23–44.

Knight Higher Education Collaborative. (2001, September). *Policy Perspectives, 10*(2), 1–9.

Konrad, A. M., & Pfeffer, J. (1991). Understanding the hiring of women and minorities in educational institutions. *Sociology of Education, 64*(3), 141–157.

Opp, R. D., & Gosetti, P. P. (2000, November 17). Promoting equity for women administrators of color. Paper presented at the annual meeting of the Association for the Study of Higher Education, Sacramento, CA (ERIC Document Reproduction Service No. ED449704).

Ross, M., & Green, M. F. (1990). The rules of the game: The unwritten code of career mobility. In K. M. Moore & S. B. Twombly (Eds.), *Administrative careers and the marketplace* (pp. 67–77). San Francisco: Jossey-Bass.

Ross, M., & Green, M. F. (2000). *The American college president: 2000 edition.* Washington, DC: American Council on Education.

Sagaria, M. D. (1988). Administrative mobility and gender: Patterns in higher education. *Journal of Higher Education*, 59(3), 305–326.

Vanderslice, R., & Litsch, K. (1998). *Women in development: Advancing women in higher education*. Weatherford: Southwestern Oklahoma State University (ERIC Document Reproduction Service No. ED444421).

3

QUALITIES OF A PRESIDENTIAL ASSISTANT

Laura Katrenicz

As you are preparing for a meeting of the governing board, which is scheduled to begin in fifteen minutes, a group of students enters the office to present the president with a letter documenting their concerns over the proposed tuition increase. As you are greeting the students, the public information officer calls to let you know that the press has received a copy of that letter and would like a comment from the president. The president just called from her car phone to let you know she has been held up in traffic due to an accident and will not return to the office for at least another half-hour.

Later that afternoon, you return to writing the institutional report you have been working on. Suddenly, you realize that the essential information from the office of a vice president promised to you a week earlier has not arrived. The report must be submitted the next day. In twenty minutes the phone rings. An irate parent demands to talk to the president about his daughter's student-teaching assignment in an inner-city school.

These examples are typical situations a presidential assistant might encounter in an average day at the office, as are the many others presented throughout this book. How each incident is handled will vary depending upon the persons involved, the culture of the institution, and other variables. However, what remain constant across each situation are the characteristics and qualities necessary for presidential assistants (PAs) to handle these situations effectively along with the countless other duties and responsibilities of the position.

In 1993, Constance Cook, then the executive assistant to the president of the University of Michigan, published an article in the *Chronicle of Higher Education* in which she discussed the qualities of an effective presidential aide. Since that time, PAs have often discussed the question of essential qualities at their annual meetings. In this chapter, I will approach this matter by exploring what features are highlighted in PA position descriptions, as exemplified by my own experiences and those of my colleagues. My intent is not to produce a definitive list of qualities, nor to refute Constance Cook (1993), nor to create yet another list of traits. Rather, I hope that by analyzing some of the more widely found facets of the position to show the range of skills and proclivities demanded by this kind of work.

A small sampling of presidential assistant job descriptions identifies many of the characteristics required of the PA by most higher education institutions. As is shown elsewhere in this volume, the PA role is one of unpredictability, vast variety, and multiple responsibilities. Many position descriptions reflect these facts. For instance, the executive assistant to the president/corporate secretary position at the Monterey Institute of International Studies calls for "strong analytical skills," while Seattle University seeks a "well-organized, self-motivated professional" with "the ability to undertake multiple priorities concurrently and independently prioritize to meet due dates/time lines." California State University, San Marcos, asks that its assistant to the president have the "ability to work in a fast-paced environment," "strong problem-solving and organizational skills," "high energy," and the "ability to work independently and as part of a team." The University of Houston, Clear Lake, executive associate to the president position requires "creativity and resourcefulness in planning and carrying out special projects and events," and flexibility in "initiating and responding to changing priorities and crisis situations."

Presidential assistants must possess many more traits in order to manage their jobs effectively and efficiently.

BEING A GOOD LISTENER

The ability to communicate effectively is crucial in all areas of academic administration. There are certain traits that enhance the PA's ability in this area. Being a good listener; having and displaying empathy, sincerity, and honesty; respect and understanding of differing perspectives; and the ability to be forthright all contribute to establishing rapport with individuals from a variety of backgrounds, regardless of age, interests, educational background, or personality type.

Anyone considering a career as a PA should make every effort to develop excellent listening skills. The president may have the luxury of not being a good listener all the time, but the assistant does not. Naturally, the job is easier if the president is a good listener, but with all he has on his plate, it sometimes is not possible to observe everything and everyone around, hear every comment made, and respond appropriately. That is where the assistant comes in. To quote a cliché, the assistant is the eyes and the ears of the president. In order to be successful in this role, PAs must acquire excellent listening skills so they can hear what the president does not hear and observe the body language that the president may overlook when in the midst of a heated discussion. Sometimes an assistant is the eyes and ears of the president because the assistant's eyes and ears see and hear things the president's never would. Regardless of how approachable a president is, there will be some staff members who will hesitate to "bother" the president with what they feel are minor issues, but they will bring those issues to the PA. Good listening skills will enable an understanding of exactly what that staff member is trying to relay, enabling the PA to relate it back to the president accurately and assist him in identifying the most appropriate response.

Good listening skills also come in handy when the assistant must act as the interpreter, stepping in to translate when members of the senior administrative team are not understanding each other, or when the president misinterprets someone's comments.

There are countless seminars and books written on the subject of effective communication. The important thing to remember is that being an effective communicator is vitally important to the success of a PA. I have found that by practicing active listening, providing consistent follow-up and honest feedback in a supportive and responsive manner, and maintaining confidentiality, I have developed trust and openness among colleagues, which has enabled me to effectively serve as the president's liaison on campus with all constituents of the college.

HONESTY AND GOOD JUDGMENT

A successful PA must have an objective view of the president and the institution and be willing to discuss these views at the proper times. (Cook discusses "good judgment and integrity.") For instance, while the assistant may not (and should not) be a "yes person," the dedication and loyalty required in a PA can sometimes result in a loss of objectivity where the president is concerned. A good PA must always remember to look at the president with a critical eye. Although this conflicts with the natural tendency to defend the president, it is a necessary tool in the effective management of a president, which is essentially what a PA does. Naturally, critiquing the president is something done only in private because in public the assistant must at all times present a united front with the president. But when the president and the assistant are alone, a good president will be looking for advice and counsel from the assistant. The assistant must maintain a suitable level of dispassion in order to provide this guidance effectively.

Honesty and judgment also come into play when presidential assistants form close ties with other staff members. It is just as important for the PA to treat faculty and staff fairly and equitably as it is for the president. The words and actions of the PA carry with them the weight of the words and actions of the president, so assistants must be especially careful not to be perceived as having "favorites" on campus. The people with whom I have established close relationships on campus are those who are acutely aware of this and refrain from putting me in positions where my credibility can be questioned.

CREDIBILITY

Credibility is a related need for an effective PA, and credibility comes from being trustworthy, honest, and forthright. Among these, being trustworthy is by far the most important quality for a PA to possess. The successful president/assistant working relationship is based on trust. The president must trust the assistant to be honest at all times, to maintain confidentiality, to always act in the president's best interests, and to almost never withhold information.[1] If the assistant (and, likewise, the president) has not demonstrated that he can be trusted, the relationship between president and assistant will be negatively affected, in turn harming the ability of the assistant to effectively serve the president.

Presidential assistants must not only prove their trustworthiness to their presidents, but must also establish that reputation with all constituents of the college. That means that the president's assistant must avoid involvement in all gossip and rumors; the role of the president's assistant, in fact, is to research the rumors and work to inform the campus of the correct information (assuming the rumors are incorrect, which so often they are).

Establishing a reputation for being trustworthy also means not repeating information that one has been asked not to repeat, and not revealing sources one is asked not to reveal. This can lead to dilemmas at times for PAs. Consider the following scenario. A dean informs the PA that one of the vice presidents has taken some action that is outside of college policy, but tells the assistant this story cannot be repeated, not even to the president. Should the assistant honor the dean's request, putting the president at risk of not addressing a situation that has the potential to cause other problems down the road? Or should she share the information with the president in the interest of the "greater good"?

There are several ways to approach such a situation. For instance, the assistant can ask the dean if the information can be shared with the president without mention of the source, or he can finagle a way to find out about what has occurred through another source, removing the dean from involvement. Or, the assistant can attempt to resolve the problem so that he only needs to report to the president that a situation occurred but that it has since been resolved. The few times I have been faced with receiving information confidentially that I felt must be shared with the president, I have been able to persuade my sources to allow me to share the information by explaining why it is important that the president know this information and assuring them that they would not be involved or affected in any way as a result. The trick is balancing the complete and open communication lines with the president and the need to honor requests for confidentiality. If the president and the assistant have established a trusting relationship, the president will trust the assistant to handle these situations with the appropriate skill and deftness.

SENSITIVITY AND DIPLOMACY

Much of that skill and deftness is defined by the degree to which the PA possesses what Seattle University describes as the "ability to work effectively with diverse audiences, with sensitivity and diplomacy." According to Saint Louis University, "tact and courtesy" are required in handling some duties. In addition to the interactions described above, there are countless other times when a PA will require sensitivity and diplomacy in order to handle a task effectively. (Cook lists "diplomatic skills" among her traits.) For instance, the assistant may be asked to inform a vice president that the president feels she should be more conscious of meeting deadlines, or may be placed in the middle of an ongoing argument between two members of the governing board. On a Monday morning, the assistant may be talking to the irate parents of the star basketball player who was disqualified from the team for misconduct, while that same afternoon the assistant may need to challenge the president on a decision not to fill a vacant administrative position, a decision the president is strongly in favor of. In each of these situations, the assistant must be sensitive to the feelings and perceptions of those he is interacting with and identify the best and most diplomatic way to approach each situation. There is no one right way to handle any of these situations. However, sensitivity and diplomacy will give the PA an edge in discovering the most appropriate methods.

ATTENTION TO DETAIL

Seattle University highlights another quality typical of PAs in its presidential assistant job description—a "keen detail-orientation and attention to accuracy." (In Cook's article, she cites "good memory and organizational skills.") The volume of correspondence, speeches, and other communications emanating from the president's office, as well as the number of brochures, annual reports, and other documents that will pass through the president's office for review, require that the PA be a perfectionist, a stickler for detail with a strong commitment to excellence. The materials that originate from the president's office are a reflection on the president. Therefore, like the president, these documents must reflect a high level of professionalism, precisely written with no grammatical or typographical errors. Appearance must be impeccable, and the information must be accurate. The PA has one of the most global perspectives on the operation of the college and is often called on to verify information or fill in gaps. Paying attention to these details is an extremely important function of the PA.

COMPOSURE

Sometimes the volume of details that pass through the PA's desk in a day can be overwhelming, as can the nature of some of those details. Seattle University looks for the "ability to act in a composed manner in challenging situations." There is no question that PAs encounter challenging situations every day (see especially the final chapter in this volume, "Juggling Jell-O: Other Duties as Assigned") and that others often look to them for guidance and leadership. The assistant must at all times maintain composure when handling the serious and even the not-so-serious crises that will arise. (Cook calls this "ability to stay cool under pressure.")

MODESTY

While there are times when the assistant will need to address a group of three hundred professionals, more often she will be writing speeches and letters of commendation, creating policies, and putting out fires for which she will receive no recognition. A certain degree of modesty is vital to performing effectively in such circumstances. Virtually everything the assistant does is done in the name of the president. She will serve on committees and attend meetings in her own right, but even then her words will be presumed to be the words of the president to some degree. That is why the assistant must always be careful to publicly support the president's position, even when she does not agree with it. And a good assistant will always make a conscious effort to promote the president. Oftentimes that will mean giving the president credit for something the assistant has accomplished (or likewise taking the blame for something the president has overlooked). For instance, when someone informs the PA that the president's speech at the previous night's dinner was a big hit with the faculty, the assistant's response should be "I enjoyed it also," rather than "Thanks, I wrote it." And when the dean of students tells the assistant he is upset because he hasn't heard back from the president on his request for additional funding, the assistant will explain to the dean how busy the president has been, and tell him that she should have made sure he responded earlier and will remind him to do so right away. (The follow-up on a situation like this is vitally important to reassuring the dean of the importance the president places on his request.)

We all have a few close friends among us who do know all that we do and all that we are responsible for. Other constituents often will fail to notice and rarely will understand the importance of the PA's role. In my opinion, a presidential assistant knows she is doing a good job when the president does not even realize all that she does. Even the most appreciative presidents will, in time, fail to recognize the many details for which the assistant is responsible once they become accustomed to having everything they need at their fingertips without asking. This can be very humbling. At the same time, the PA must also have a great deal of self-confidence to understand that a lack of recognition in this case is actually a sign of a job well done. (Cook states that a "strong self image" is important as one tries to remain in the background and take solace in one's own sense of achievement.)

LOYALTY

Tied into all of these qualities described in this chapter is the trait most necessary in a PA, and that is loyalty. (Cook lists "loyalty to the president and his/her agenda.") The presidential assistant must have the capacity for sincere and dedicated loyalty. If the PA has a fundamental loyalty to the president, all the other pieces that comprise a positive working relationship between president and assistant will fall into place. That loyalty drives the assistant to always operate in the president's best interest, to be supportive of the president's initiatives, to be critical of the president (in private) when necessary, and to do whatever possible to protect and promote the president's image among all constituents.

LAST BUT NOT LEAST

Two final qualities may be needed to make it through the first day in such a job. As the University of Houston, Clear Lake, presidential assistant job description states, have a sense of humor, and, as Mark Curchack of Arcadia University says, have a "tolerance for ambiguity . . . anyone who likes it all neat and tidy is in the wrong business." Without a sense of humor and a healthy love of the unknown, a PA will never be able to juggle all the tasks, manage all the responsibilities, interact effectively with all the constituents, and handle all the never-before-seen situations that arise each day without burnout. (Cook calls these traits "tolerance for ambiguity and tolerance for risk taking.")

No such list of qualities or traits can presume to be exhaustive. Each presidential assistant position has its own peculiarities, and the variety among positions is substantial. I hope that by discussing several of the common dimensions of the role, as confirmed by the earlier writing of Constance Cook, I have portrayed the central qualities that successful PAs must possess.

NOTE

1. There are situations of conflict or grievance where it may be incorrect to inform the president too early, or at all. If the president serves as the final appeal in a chain of appeals, it might compromise the president to know details too early

in the process. Other situations may make it awkward to inform the president, as exemplified later in this chapter.

REFERENCE

Cook, Constance. (1993, July 7). Gatekeeper, facilitator, gofer, flunky? How to be an effective presidential aide. *Chronicle of Higher Education*, B3.

4

MANAGING THE PRESIDENT'S OFFICE

Marc Schaeffer

There is a popular cartoon that is all too familiar to most folks involved in any sort of managerial or administrative work. It depicts a rather frantic individual with only his or her head showing, flailing about while immersed in water surrounded by thick weeds and bushes and threatened on all sides by angry, sharp-toothed creatures. The sanitized version of the caption reads: "It is difficult to remember that the objective is to drain the swamp when you are up to your neck in alligators." This image rings profoundly true for presidential assistants (PAs) because we consistently struggle with finding a workable balance between proactive leadership and oversight of the president's office and the compelling "crisis management" reaction to the multitude of urgent issues impinging on the president and his or her staff each day. Although the reality of the job of PA may mean that the swamp is never completely drained, it should be possible to devise, implement, and refine an ongoing "swamp improvement and development" plan that represents a thoughtful, reasoned, and organized effort to lead and manage rather than merely react.

The management and organizational theory literature is teeming with definitions and theories of management (typing "theories of management" into the Google search engine produced nearly three thousand hits), but when in doubt, I always start with Webster's Dictionary. "Management" is defined therein as "the act, manner or practice of managing, supervising or controlling . . . executive skill." Perhaps more colloquially, one might define management as "doing what's necessary to get a job done." Histories of management have classified management systems as "classical," "bureaucratic," "scientific," and "administrative." More contemporary perspectives incorporate "systems theory," "contingency views," "quality," and "chaos theory" (see, e.g., Miles, 1975). Although thought-provoking and useful to provide alternative conceptual frameworks for understanding management systems, these theories do little to help one get a handle on the day-to-day problems surrounding the people and resources necessary to carry out the activities associated with effectively and efficiently managing the president's office. More useful are the so-called six functions of management represented by the acronym POSLED—planning, organizing, staffing, leading, evaluating, and developing (Quehl, 1978)—and the four "frames" for interpreting the events of organizational life—structural, human resources, political, and symbolic (Bolman & Deal, 1985).

ORGANIZATIONAL "FRAMES"

We are all familiar with the cliché about people who see the glass as half-full or half-empty. This refers, of course, to the unavoidable human inclination to impose on "reality" (i.e., the degree of fullness of the glass) a perspective (the contemporary word is "spin") not inherent in the phenomena being observed (after all, the glass has a finite and measurable volume of liquid), but rather derived from the history, attitudes, disposition, and desires of the observer. The notion that "reality" is a social construct—that what people come to believe about the events in their lives is, at least in part, dependent on something within them and is derived from interaction with others—is absolutely critical to understanding management and leadership, and particularly so in higher education where so much that occurs is so equivocal. In fact, I submit that the approach one takes and the decisions one makes in managing the president's office are a direct result of the perspective, or "frame" through which the PA and the president view the work that is to occur there. Bolman and Deal (1985) said it more succinctly: "It is commonplace that different people see things differently. It is less widely understood that differences in theory can create differences in reality" (p. 20).

A brief example is illustrative of the different perspectives represented by the four frames as well as the practical implications of the impact of the particular frame through which one "sees" events on the administrative and managerial actions that one would be inclined to employ in addressing the issue. About fifteen years ago a dean of students and a vice president for administration and finance (neither of whom is still in those positions at this institution) had a disagreement about the use by students of an out-of-service tennis court for roller-skating. The court was out of service because its asphalt surface was too damaged for playing tennis. The dean argued that there was no other place on campus that this activity could occur without interrupting other activities or posing a danger to students or passersby and that the campus was woefully lacking in overall informal recreation space. The vice president argued that roller-skating would make it more costly to restore the courts for tennis and that the damaged surface exposed the university to liability if students were allowed to use it. A *structural* perspective on this conflict would focus on the proper locus of organizational decision making regarding student recreation and campus maintenance, the rules that govern informal recreation, and the facts associated with the condition of the courts, the legal risk of liability, the cost of future damage from roller-skating, and the comparative cost to repair the courts or secure suitable alternate recreation space. A *human resources* perspective always focuses on the relationships between the people involved in any issue. Can the dean and the VP find a way to work this out without requiring intervention by the president, to whom they both report? Does the conflict create animosity between their respective staffs, who have to work together on other issues? Does their desire for the president to make a decision for them affect their relationship with the president? How does this conflict influence their work on other issues of shared responsibility? A *political* orientation examines issues from the perspective of the power of the participants, the various constituencies likely to align themselves on either side, and the self-interests of those constituencies affected by the decision. Who has the power to make this decision? What is the impact of the student government association pressing for a decision in the favor of the roller-skating group? If one or the other side "gives in" on this issue, what will be the consequence (accumulation or expenditure of political capital) for the next issue about which they disagree? If roller-skating is permitted on the courts, will students with other informal recreational interests claim entitlement to some support as well? Finally, a *symbolic* frame of reference focuses on shaping the meaning inferred by observers from the ambiguous events of organizational life. From this perspective, roller-skating is not merely recreation. It represents student autonomy, perceived support for student needs over administrative interests, and a statement about institutional priorities. For the VP, in the symbolic sense, this issue is about the institution's commitment to cost effectiveness, risk aversion, and prudence in the management of physical resources and the manifest consequences of unaddressed deferred maintenance. Obviously, complicated issues involving diverse individuals typically present themselves with attributes of some or all of the four "frames." Bensimon, Neumann, and Birnbaum (1989) describe the capacity to "see things" from multiple perspectives as "cognitive complexity," and in fact show in their research on college presidents that the capacity to do so is a discernible quality of more effective leaders.

I fully recognize that none of the foregoing offers any utilitarian advice concerning the considerable volume and complexity of tasks required to manage a president's office. Given that nearly 70 percent of respondents to the NAPAHE Survey of Presidential Assistants (hereafter referred to as "the survey") report "total" or "some" responsibility for "office administration," this sort of advice is certainly important. What I believe is vital to understand, however, is that how one "sees" an issue determines how one organizes and acts to address and resolve issues.

Let me suggest, then, a simple framework for categorizing and organizing the many tasks necessary to manage the modern president's office, augmented by the implicit understanding that the "frames" through which the PA and the others who come into contact with the president's office "see" the tangible and intangible results of these efforts will profoundly affect their meaning and perceived effectiveness.

SIX FUNCTIONS OF MANAGEMENT

I now turn to the six management functions captured by the acronym PO-SLED—planning, organizing, staffing, leading, evaluating, and developing. Planning is the process of determining what should be done. Organizing is arranging the means to carry out what is planned. Staffing is recruiting, appointing, training, and retaining individuals with the requisite skills, motivation, and inclination to contribute to the fulfillment of the plan. A comprehensive definition of leadership fills wings of business and organizational psychology libraries, but the tasks of communicating with and motivating others to work collaboratively toward development or fulfillment of plans is a useful, albeit abbreviated version. Evaluating is essentially measuring the extent of attainment of stated plans and their associated objectives and reviewing the performance of the personnel employed to accomplish those plans and objectives. Finally, developing is providing the programs and services that allow employees to grow in their professional capacities. Important to note, particularly for presidential office staff, is that professional development must include so-called hard skills (how to perform specific substantive tasks) and soft skills, the interpersonal skills necessary to work well with others and to develop a sense of occasion appropriate to their role and position.

PLANNING AND ORGANIZING

In chapter 8 of this book on the roles and responsibilities of the secretary to the board of trustees, Nancy Kelly writes: "The day-to-day work life of an assistant to the president can be about triage, about a steady stream of small emergencies that, once resolved, keep things running smoothly." Resolving small emergencies may indeed be a part of every day, and for some may be what keeps the job of PA interesting and invigorating (for others perhaps frustrating and stressful); but thinking ahead; creating appropriate structure; managing relationships; identifying and mobilizing influential constituencies in support of institutional policies; shaping and conveying desired meaning to internal and external constituents; and seeking, training, and developing staff with the skills and sensitivities to work in this environment with this particular president surely represent some of our days. Indeed, these efforts may even serve to prevent or moderate some of those emergencies and are, in the long term, at least as important as making the trains run on time. Effective accomplishment of all this is important if one is to "keep things running smoothly."

Over 50 percent of survey respondents indicate that their job is "conceived as senior management or professional." Over 65 percent report "interacting with the governing board." Over 55 percent report holding a degree or doing academic work at or beyond the master's level. Individuals with these responsibilities and with this stature expect of themselves, and their institutions need from them, more than triage. This is why planning and organizing should be part of the work of every PA. The survey of PAs suggests that many of them indeed do these things. About 63 percent of respondents report that they have "total" or "some" responsibility for "establishing agendas for policy groups." Nearly 66 percent report that they have "total" or "some" responsibility for "coordinating policy with senior officials." About 80 percent of PAs indicate that they "coordinate special projects" and about 70 percent report that they "coordinate special events." In fact, nearly all of the responsibilities of PAs enumerated in the survey require planning and organizing. Notwithstanding all the types of planning described in the planning literature (e.g., long-range planning, strategic planning, tactical planning, budget planning), managing the president's office requires a "planful" approach to two different kinds of issues.

The first might be described as "process" planning. Most president's offices are directly responsible for many activities and processes, such as trustee meetings, commencement, all kinds of personnel actions, and various campus events that require (or are required by union contract) to occur at specific points in time. Sketching out a calendar for the key tasks and deadlines required to accomplish the various steps in these processes well in advance, and communicating those deadlines widely to the offices that must contribute their parts of those steps is a simple kind of planning that can be very helpful in organizing the work of the office staff toward accomplishing the final product. As described in great detail in chapter 8, this kind of planning is particularly important when the time and attention of board members are involved. Also, knowing that the president attends certain out-of-town meetings each year, and knowing where those meetings are located well in advance, allows the development staff to prearrange meetings with key alums, donors, politicians, and other sources of potential favorable influence for the university who live in those cities. Good planning would suggest that every event or process for which the president's office has primary functional responsibility have a task chart and associated timelines sketched out well in advance. Organizing this kind of effort involves not only determining all the activities and processes to track, but assuring the awareness and participation of necessary staff, both within and outside the president's office, required to carry out the necessary tasks.

Organizing the never-ending flow of correspondence that enters and leaves the president's office is also an important management task. Although various styles and technologies are available, the objective must be to assure the accurate and timely response, delegation, sharing with appropriate staff, filing, and follow-up to all communications received. PAs must develop an instinct for the sources or subjects of correspondence to which the president wishes to reply in his or her name, and for how much and about what a president wants to know, and must assure that the right response or information, at the right level of detail, from the right person and at the right time is provided. This is clearly an area in which a president's organizational "frame" comes into play, and the PA must take that into account. A president for whom relationships among senior administrators is a central focus, for example, must be briefed promptly about any interactions that may adversely influence those relationships. A president who views administrative organization through a structural frame, however, might consider such information irrelevant, but would be interested in a minor organizational realignment two levels deep in one of the institution's divisions.

Organizing the financial affairs of the president's office is also an essential task. A president's spending is a sensitive issue both internally and externally. Records must be maintained that demonstrate fiscal integrity and prudence and are strictly in compliance with institutional and governmental policies. Many institutions employ a staff member with the responsibility for internal auditing. Where that exists, it should be made clear and widely known that regular audits of the president's office budget and spending practices are expected. Where it does not, the PA should work with the president and the business services unit to provide a responsible means whereby the institutional board or system governance body is assured that someone is monitoring the president's spending, just as the spending of other campus units is monitored.

A second kind of planning is required for the development, selection, and implementation of new initiatives. Only someone with a purely reactive posture would suggest doing the same things the same way every year. Working with the president, the PA may develop new activities that promote the goals and objectives of the office and the institution. For example, this past year I sought to further the unfiltered contact of the president with students. Prompted by the suggestion of a NAPAHE colleague, and working in concert with the student services staffs, we created "Pizza with the President" nights in each residence hall. Although we heard our share of familiar complaints, the vast majority of the participants felt positively that they had a chance to communicate directly and personally with the president without intervening layers of staff. The efforts of staff to organize these events and the follow-up on issues raised by students was not insignificant. The key point is that a planning mentality can serve both to improve the effectiveness and efficiency of routine processes and events (and in doing so minimize the need for triage) but also stimulate the creation of new activities that promote a positive image of the president's office and further the mission of the institution. It serves us well to remember that those who are most directly involved with and affected by the activities in which the president's office takes leadership will interpret these activities according to their particular "frame," and therefore savvy planning will consider the message that may be received, as well as the message intended to be sent.

STAFFING AND DEVELOPING

Just over 37 percent of respondents to the survey report that the clerical staff of the president's office in which they work totals three or more. Whether a large or small staff, the issue of the proper mix and abilities of personnel represents a critical element in managing any president's office. The specific functions and tasks carried out by a president's office are dependent upon the size of the president's staff and the institution, its particular organizational structure, the relationships between and among administrative officers, and the leadership and managerial styles of the president. In a small office, all staff must be generally familiar with all tasks, even though each staff member may have a specific assignment. In a larger office, task specialization is more likely, but some cross-training serves both the professional development of the staff and the capacity of the office to function when staff are away or depart.

Because of the importance and sensitivity of issues that come to the president's office, the appearance, demeanor, attitude, sensitivity, and task proficiency of staff are particularly critical. These same requirements apply to any student workers hired to assist regular staff. The president's office must project the most professional image possible due to the "high stakes" issues that arrive at its door. Administrative and clerical mistakes, as well as misjudgments in dealing with people, must be studiously minimized. Staff must, by nature, be scrupulously attentive to all matters of detail and must be encouraged to maintain a high level of concentration when undertaking all projects requiring accuracy of detail.

Whoever is responsible for the president's calendar must be able to handle both the high-volume and detail-oriented work associated with presidential travel and service on countless committees and commissions, as well as the sensitivity of the issue of who gets on the calendar and when.

Visitors to the president's office, particularly those from the private sector or government, expect to see both people and decor looking polished and welcoming but not ostentatious. When the *Chronicle of Higher Education* reported on the governance difficulties at Adelphi University in the late 1990s, it noted that the president's office was luxuriously appointed and had a security system requiring that anyone seeking entry be buzzed in through locked doors. Most PAs (on their good days) would probably conclude that this style does not project an open and welcoming attitude to faculty, staff, and visitors, nor send the proper signal to a budget-stressed campus. Employees must be neatly dressed in business attire, professionally friendly, courteous, and upbeat. A sense of humor is vital, but just as important is good judgment about when and when not to display it. They must present themselves as informed about issues and guests who may arrive, and thus the PA must have an ongoing mechanism for assuring that information needed by staff flows freely to them. They must be generally familiar with matters of institutional culture, protocol, and heightened sensitivity on campus.

While staff need to know a great deal to avoid surprises or mistakes, they must be exceptionally conscious of the necessity for confidentiality. While not every issue they may confront or document that crosses their desk will be obviously confidential (like personnel matters), they must possess or develop excellent judgment and self-discipline about not discussing office business with their colleagues elsewhere on campus. One of my colleagues related to me a recent experience in her office in which a student assistant was talking with a newspaper reporter about university business—clearly not a strategy featured in the media relations handbook.

Institutions with a commitment to diversity as part of their mission must be particularly sensitive to recruiting and retaining staff with the ethnic and gender makeup that models this commitment. A president cannot argue persuasively for the importance of ethnic and gender diversity in faculty and administration when visitors find only white male professionals and white female clerical staff in the president's office. Frequently, the human resources unit will conduct university-wide staff development and performance evaluation programs and processes to which staff in the president's office will have access and will be subjected. The PA must assure that those processes allow for inclusion of the kinds of technical and interpersonal skills and sensitivities that are required in the president's office.

LEADING AND EVALUATING

The roles of leadership and evaluation are linked in successfully managing the president's office because leadership entails enticing folks to work together toward shared goals, and evaluation reveals if and how well they are getting there. Whatever definition or understanding of leadership resonates most clearly for each of us, we exercise that leadership in our work off and on campus, both within and outside the president's office. About 27 percent of respondents to the survey indicated that they hold line responsibilities, and thus exercise leadership in defining the goals and objectives of the units they oversee. Since the focus here is on managing the president's office, I will address the elements of leadership that the PA may exercise within the office itself. Through whatever frame, leadership on the part of the PA in managing the president's office involves taking the initiative to translate the president's style and directives into administrative and programmatic activities, communicating with staff and eliciting feedback about how best to do this, finding ways to motivate staff to give their best efforts, rewarding them however possible when they do so, and modeling the behavior and demeanor appropriate to the setting. Evaluating requires an assessment, both formally and anecdotally, of the effectiveness of these efforts.

As a devotee of *Star Trek* in its many incarnations, I am reminded of the oft-repeated words of Captain John Luc Picard who, when presented with a complicated policy or engineering option by his officers with which he concurred, would say, "Make it so." I am sure we have all experienced that phone call or e-mail from the president indicating that he or she has just made a commitment that this, that, or the next thing will be in place by next Tuesday, and the PA should please "make it so." Staff efforts to carry out very general programmatic directives require leadership from the PA to assure that the directive is clearly understood, to break down the task into manageable parts, to delegate those parts to appropriately skilled staff, to oversee and guide implementation of the various parts, and to assure that the sum of the parts ultimately constitutes the desired whole. Presidents should rarely be told something can't be done, but good leadership on the part of the PA requires that the PA be open and candid about the potential institutional consequences of presidential intentions as well as any extraordinary administrative or logistical challenges that stand in the way. The nuances of the ideal relationship between the PA and the president are beyond the scope of this chapter, but suffice to say that the PA's willingness and capacity to tell the president his or her perception of the "truth," in strict confidence and with the appropriate demeanor and deference, are among the most important yet necessarily unseen leadership qualities of the PA.

While most staff find working in the president's office challenging, inter-esting, and rewarding, it can also be experienced as confusing, demanding, and stressful. The PA must exercise leadership to help staff maximize the former and minimize the latter. Teamwork is built on honest communi-cation of issues and expectations, unfailing treatment of all people with respect, and conscious efforts to recognize commitment, hard work, and success. Work in the president's office does not always occur according to a rigid schedule. Staff sometimes must come early and stay late. To the extent that doing so does not create other problems (e.g., the perception by others of favorable treatment for the president's staff), the PA can allow for some schedule flexibility for staff during less busy times, knowing that the next busy time isn't far away. Informal social amenities like celebrating birthdays, holiday lunches, impromptu "coffee and muffins" on a Friday morning, and other climate-enhancing touches build rapport between and among staff, and that good feeling translates into more productive teamwork. Finally, although some people experience a job well done as its own reward, it still feels good to hear someone in a leadership position say "good job." Staff who feel valued and respected translate that feeling into better work habits and less acting out and as a result exercise more initiative. While it may not sound like "leadership" with a capital "L," these little things can make a big difference in the functioning of the president's office.

Evaluation need not only take the form of formal survey instruments seeking feedback from service recipients as to their satisfaction and recommendations for improvement. Although new programs developed and overseen by the PA may benefit from this kind of structured evaluation, to paraphrase New York Yankees catcher and wordsmith Yogi Berra, "You can learn a lot just by listening." Finding the right moment to ask folks who interact with the president's office how they feel about those interactions can yield fruitful information. Students call the president's office for many reasons, but more often than not they are frustrated by some aspect of the bureaucracy and feeling at the end of their ropes. If as PAs we have the responsibility to manage those interactions (either directly or by carefully arranged referral), asking those students how they felt they were treated when they called is a good barometer for how other, less frustrated callers may be treated. Similarly, a staff "debriefing" after some major event organized by the president's office is a useful way to get feedback while the experience is still fresh, elicit suggestions for improvement for the next time, and demonstrate to staff that their contributions and input are valued. As part of whatever performance appraisal process is conducted for staff, a candid discussion with each staff member individually about how his or her interaction with the PA is perceived, how he or she thinks the office is working, what could be done better or differently, and what professional development activities would serve the mutual interests of the employee and the institution is another important element of an evaluation program.

FINAL THOUGHTS

The responsibility of the presidential assistant in managing the president's office is important for two distinct reasons: first, from an operational point of view, because the work of the president is vital to the progress and success of the institution and the capacity of the president to do his or her job is directly affected by the effectiveness and efficiency of the president's office; second, because the *perception* formed by the board of trustees or system governing body, the campus, and the external community as to the performance of the president is affected both substantively and symbolically by the opinion those constituencies form of the president's staff.

Success in managing the president's office involves attaining the "cognitive complexity" to see issues and help others see them through multiple "frames," and to understand the particular perspectives that others are bringing to bear on complex issues. It involves attention to the functions (and others) discussed under the headings of planning, organizing, staffing, leading, evaluating, and developing. Also, try to avoid the alligators!

REFERENCES

Bensimon, E., Neumann, A., & Birnbaum, R. (1989). *Making sense of administrative leadership: The "l" word in higher education.* Washington, DC: ASHE-ERIC Higher Education Reports (report #1).

Bolman, L. G., & Deal, T. E. (1985). *Modern approaches to understanding and managing organizations.* San Francisco: Jossey-Bass.

Miles, R. E. (1975). *Theories of management: Implications for organizational behavior and development.* New York: McGraw-Hill.

Quehl, G. H. (Ed.). (1978). *Handbook for college administration.* Washington, DC: Council for the Advancement of Small Colleges.

MANAGING THE LIFE OF THE PRESIDENT

Antoinette G. Gifford[1]

Managing a president's schedule is one of the most arduous responsibilities of the presidential office. In some cases the task falls directly to the presidential assistant, while in others the PA has general calendar oversight with most of the work resting with another staff person. Calendar management is more art than science, requiring both knowing what is most important and understanding the conditions under which the president best leads. Presidents, assistants, and institutions are different, and, therefore, strategies that may work well in one situation may not work well in others. Regardless of circumstance, the assistant must spend enough time with the president to understand his or her habits, priorities, and leadership style. Where possible, new presidential assistants are wise to study their presidents in action, taking note of the situations in which they are at their very best. Good communication between the president and the assistant is also important, especially at the beginning of their working relationship.

IN THE BEGINNING

At every institution, there are annual or periodic events that every president must participate in or attend. While some of these are ceremonial, such as orientation receptions or alumni recognition ceremonies, others are central to the governance of the institution. Those new to the academic enterprise should remember that the tradition of shared governance places distinct demands on the president's time and cannot or should not be ignored. For new assistants (or, for that matter, presidents), it is critical to identify just what those events are by consulting with long-standing staff who are more familiar with the rhythms of the college or university. Some of the events common to most institutions include, but are not limited to: faculty governance meetings; senior staff meetings; meetings with the board of trustees, managers, or overseers; convocations, orientations, and completion exercises; and homecoming and alumni events. If the campus is part of a larger system, there will be additional meetings with the central office and its oversight body.

Successful time management also requires an understanding of the culture at the local institution, such as whether there is an expectation that the president be highly visible. In larger institutions, for instance, where schools and academic programs operate in a loosely coupled federation, there are frequently lower expectations regarding presidential engagement. One must also consider how the president's personal style matches with these expectations. A more charismatic leader may prefer the use of larger events to convey his or her message and build momentum for that vision. Others, in turn, may prefer midsize or small group meetings with constituents.

In addition to the internal events that form the foundation of the president's schedule, calendar managers must consider the external obligations of the president. Most presidents serve on local boards or participate in local affairs and many participate in national, or even international, organizations. In an American Council on Education survey of presidents, more than 40 percent identified community relations as one of their four primary roles and responsibilities (Ross & Green, 2000, p. 27). Not every community event requires the personal involvement of the president, however. For some events, having the assistant or another senior staff member represent the institution will suffice. Understanding which events may be delegated and encouraging the president to delegate when possible will help the assistant maximize the time the president can spend on matters that do require his or her personal attention.

Together, these internal and external events form the framework for the president's calendar and, to some extent, define how his or her time is balanced. The number of routine obligations can quickly outstrip the actual time available and squeeze out more important, but less urgent, tasks. From time to time, it may be necessary for the assistant to help the president evaluate whether there are some external commitments that have fulfilled their purpose and may be left behind. The assistant should also keep in mind that internal obligations can limit the president's ability to serve the institution by dealing with external constituents. Although the details of the president's engagements may need to stay confidential, most faculty and staff members are likely to understand the necessity of the president's missing an internal function to attend to pressing external matters. Likewise, external constituents can appreciate the assistant's candor in communicating the limits on a president's time. In both cases, the credibility of the assistant is crucial to maintaining a good rapport for the future.

MATTERS OF INSTITUTIONAL DIFFERENCE

Beyond the core meetings and appointments, presidential assistants must use their sensibilities about the president's priorities and initiatives to balance the remaining part of the workday. Presidential assistants are uniquely situated to forecast which opportunities best advance the president's agenda. Priorities vary from institution to institution and will change over the course of the presidency. Regardless of what priorities emerge, the president's calendar should always be considered as a means to advance the president's goals (Weingartner, 1996). It requires diligence to maintain long-term priorities in the face of constant and sudden demands on the president's time.

Presidential tenure will also play a role in assessing the need for certain activities; new presidents may find a greater need for establishing relationships on campus, pressing for a more internally focused schedule (Astin & Scherrei, 1980). Consider one president at a small college who early in her administration committed herself to meeting every member of the faculty during a series of small lunches. Senior presidents or those who have delegated faculty relations to the chief academic officer may, in turn, have more limited engagements with faculty, instead focusing on advancement or other priorities.

In practice, a common arrangement at many colleges and universities is for assistants to review all invitations or meeting requests and sort them according to need or according to the president's priorities. Once arranged, possibly with notations regarding competing obligations, the proposed calendar and items are forwarded to the president for review and final decisions. Another common strategy, particularly for on-campus meeting requests, is for the presidential assistant to collect as much information as possible about the request to ensure that the president's, and not some other campus administrator's, attention is required.

Aside from invitations, presidential assistants can also focus the president's time through a careful review of all incoming mail. Typically, an assistant can anticipate the additional steps or information required to respond to all correspondence.

Assistants also need to remain mindful of how far in advance and how fully the calendar is booked. For example, one PA noted that he never schedules more than half of the president's time over a week in advance. In this way, time is always available for preparation, follow-up, and addressing last-minute emergencies. Many PAs create time limits for administrative meetings to ensure that the day moves smoothly. Others balance the president's time by designating days for the exclusive use of either internal or external activities. Seasoned PAs can further plan the president's day to best advantage by scheduling difficult or challenging meetings during particular times of the day. For example, presidents who are early birds might be best served by situating office work time or senior management meetings early in the morning. Other presidents may value "buffer time" in between difficult meetings to allow them to refocus, or may require unstructured time to think, dream, or simply roam the campus in search of revitalization and inspiration.

In addition to planning how the president's day is spent, PAs can, and often do, manage the president's time through advanced preparation for meetings. That is, by gathering germane information in advance—through discussion or in writing—the PA can focus the agenda and shorten the duration of meetings, particularly those with internal constituencies. (In some cases the PA may choose to write a literal agenda for such meetings to ensure that all of the required topics are covered in a minimum of time.) It is worth noting that the process of gathering information is multidirectional. So in addition to gaining the right information for the leader, PAs can also serve presidents by helping other meeting participants understand the likely questions and types of information that might be needed to address the topic at hand.

It is common for presidential assistants to synthesize information, analyze data, and make suggestions or recommendations to the president. Any time the assistant spends on such tasks is well worthwhile when it allows the president to make a quicker or better decision. In some cases the assistant may sit on a campus committee as a representative of the president. This participation can help to frame the results of the committee's work by adding an institutional perspective to the deliberations while allowing other committee members to speak more freely than they might in the presence of the president. It also allows the president to see pros and cons in ways that are not apparent from reports, since the assistant can share the nature of the deliberations, and not just outcomes, with the president.

A responsibility related to scheduling is that of dealing with students, faculty, or staff who call or walk in demanding the attention of the president without going through proper procedures. Unless the president has an open-door policy, it requires a combination of institutional knowledge, patience, and tact (and sometimes a bit of nerve) to defuse the situation and redirect the person appropriately. Even in those rare cases when the most expeditious step is for the person to see the president, the assistant may minimize the impact on the president's schedule by getting as much background information as possible and discreetly briefing the president on the facts of the case. Another helpful strategy may be to have the person put the complaint in writing before seeing the president. This gives the person and the institution a record of the exact complaint and allows additional time to assess how best to proceed.

Although the topic of presidential assistants and speechwriting is addressed at greater length in another chapter, it should be noted that chief executives will have far-ranging habits regarding preparing for speeches. I am reminded of one executive who was a natural speaker. Sharp and witty, he could deliver a thirty-minute speech with just two pages of notes providing an overall frame for his remarks and some facts or an engaging story or quote suitable for the topic. As staff, we were convinced that we were obligated to provide more preparation for important engagements. Over time we came to realize that the more we wrote ahead of time or rehearsed with him, the worse he sounded—stiff, wooden, and completely disconnected from the delivery of his remarks. After one particularly poor showing, we finally realized short preparation worked best for him and that we needed to adapt to his needs rather than our expectations.

Unquestionably, fund-raising has become a dominant responsibility for modern college presidents at both private and public institutions. An American Council on Education survey showed that while resource development was not deemed the most important role for presidents, it on average consumed more than a third of the president's time (Ross & Green, 2000). Given the current economic climate both for foundations that typically support higher education and state budgets, this figure is likely to grow in the near future. In thinking about the president's schedule, the assistant must constantly keep in mind that the time spent should have some relationship to the possible revenue stream. At most institutions, the advancement or development office works closely with the president's staff to schedule advancement activities.

One particular challenge for college presidents is the propensity to become so overcommitted with meetings that there is little solitary time to do the other work needed to preside. In our office, experience has shown that preparation and solitary work time cannot be left waiting for periods of free time. Rather, we actively build into the schedule office hours to return phone calls, respond to campus issues, plan, and coordinate. In order to use this time productively, we find that the president needs blocks of at least an hour in length.

INTO THE LATE HOURS

The work of the college president extends well past the regular workday with social obligations that maintain external relations and advance the institution. If the president is married, communication between the spouse and the PA may be particularly important. A new PA may want to request a meeting with the spouse to determine the best system for communication, be it by phone, e-mail, notes "sent home" with the president, or some other method. One PA regularly prints a copy of the president's calendar for the spouse to double-check evening and weekend engagements, while another makes sure the spouse has access to the president's scheduling software to view the calendar directly. In addition to keeping the spouse informed, the PA may need to ascertain which events the spouse will attend with the president.

Presidents often hold official social events in their own homes. Traditionally, much of the planning and work related to these events has been relegated to the president's spouse. However, with the emergence of more female presidents—now just shy of 20 percent of all American college presidents (Ross & Green, 2000)—and more spouses having independent professional lives, more of the social responsibilities of the presidency fall to presidential assistants. It is then the responsibility of the assistant to determine what level of consultation, if any, will be required with the president or the spouse on the details of the event. While in some cases the nimble PA has full responsibility, in other institutions, particularly those of some size, these efforts are shared with an events coordinator. This task carries a wide range of responsibilities, from coordinating the guest list to planning the menu to thinking about what message is being conveyed at the event. All of this requires careful planning, creativity, and a clear understanding of the president's goals, along with a touch of diplomacy.

The stated and implicit objectives of the event are the first issue to consider in planning. For example, a homecoming dinner might provide ample opportunity to court current and potential donors who are also sports fans. In assembling the guest list, the PA will also want to include other members of the college community who can speak to the college's objectives. Thus a dinner where the implicit motive is securing support for the expansion of the science center might include the dean overseeing that area or a notable faculty member who could speak eloquently of the benefits of the potential improvement. For those PAs at public institutions, it is important to remember that a generous sprinkling of elected officials may be crucial.

In thinking about the tone of the event, it is important to consider the expectations of the prospective guests, in addition to the style of the president. While some donors expect to be attended to lavishly, others consider such treatment a poor use of the resources they have made available. Until a PA has acquired the experience or the records to show which category guests fall into, consultation with the president or advancement staff may serve as a guide. Even in those cases where PAs are not responsible for the event itself, they are often asked to aid the president during the event to ensure that needed interactions occur. For very large receptions, one PA prepares a small cue card or checklist of high-profile guests whom the president should be sure to greet before the evening is out. Another strategy is to have the president stay close to the entrance for the opening part of the event to assure an opportunity to greet every guest personally.

NOTE

1. With assistance from Mona Rankin, executive vice president, former executive assistant to the president, State University of New York, Old Westbury; Carrie Stefaniak, executive assistant to the chancellor, University of Arkansas; Eileen Sullivan, dean of students, Elmhurst College, former executive assistant to the president/policy analyst, Bowling Green State University.

REFERENCES AND FURTHER READING

Astin, A. W., & Scherrei, R. A. (1980). *Maximizing leadership effectiveness* (1st ed.). San Francisco: Jossey-Bass.

Birnbaum, R. (1992). *How academic leadership works: Understanding success and failure in the academic presidency.* San Francisco: Jossey-Bass.

Cote, L. S. (1985). The relative importance of presidential roles. *Journal of Higher Education, 56*(6), 664–676.

Fisher, J. L. (1988). How presidents can wield power. *AGB Reports*, *20*(5), 20–24.

Geiger, R. L. (1992). The historical matrix of American higher education. In R. L. Geiger (Ed.), *History of higher education annual*. University Park: Higher Education Program, Pennsylvania State University.

Johnstone, D. B. (1997). The United States. In M. F. Green (Ed.), *Transforming higher education: Views from leaders around the world* (pp. 133–149). Phoenix, AZ: American Council on Education and Oryx Press.

Kelly, F. J. (1991). Evolution in leadership in American higher education: A changing paradigm. *Journal for Higher Education Management*, *7*(1), 29–34.

Kerr, C. (1996). *The uses of the university* (4th ed.). Cambridge, MA: Harvard University Press.

Kerr, C., & Gade, M. L. (1987). The contemporary college president. *American Scholar*, *56*(1), 29–44.

Millett, J. D. (1980). *Management, governance, and leadership: A guide for college and university administrators*. New York: Amacom.

Ross, M., & Green, M. F. (2000). *The American college president: 2000 edition*. Washington, DC: American Council on Education.

Shapiro, H. T. (1998). University presidents—then and now. In H. T. Shapiro & W. G. Bowen (Eds.), *Universities and their leadership* (pp. 65–99). Princeton, NJ: Princeton University Press.

Weingartner, R. H. (1996). *Fitting form to function*. Phoenix, AZ: American Council on Education and Oryx Press.

PRESIDENTIAL ASSISTANTS AND INSTITUTIONAL ADVANCEMENT

Marcus Lingenfelter and Michael R. McGreevey

The important role of college and university presidents in institutional advancement has been extensively researched, examined, and well documented by higher education scholars and the Council for Advancement and Support of Education (CASE). However, the role presidential assistants (PAs) play in this important administrative arena has gone largely unnoticed, until recently.

The research for a doctoral dissertation by Toni Gifford (a former PA herself) documents the extraordinary level to which PAs are involved in the various aspects of institutional advancement (personal communication). Moreover, the topic has been a favorite on the National Association of Presidential Assistants in Higher Education (NAPAHE) annual meeting agenda for the last decade. Two articles in CASE's *CURRENTS* magazine, written by Marcus Lingenfelter, argued that PAs are institutional advancement partners and, as such, should be embraced by full-time practitioners of the trade. Therefore, this chapter will serve as a primer on institutional advancement as well as a guide for effective PA involvement in this ever more critical area of higher education administration.

IMPORTANCE OF INSTITUTIONAL ADVANCEMENT TO PAS

Because a PA is both a generalist by nature and a personal extension of the president by position, it is admittedly difficult to produce a clear definition of the "typical" PA. The roles largely depend upon four factors: (1) the needs of the president; (2) institutional size, scope, and mission; (3) education, experience, and talents of the individual; and (4) current issues or specific needs of the institution. Out of those factors come positional responsibilities that most commonly include managing the operations of the president's office (e.g., scheduling, correspondence, speechwriting, constituent relations), staffing the governing board, coordinating special events and presidential initiatives or projects, and generally supporting the president.

Since institutional advancement is a primary responsibility and concern of the president, then it becomes at least a de facto concern for all PAs. Moreover, the tasks commonly performed by PAs have become more influenced, involved, and even intertwined with those of institutional advancement. So perhaps it is time to add "advancement officer" to the list of presidential assistant descriptors.

WHAT IS INSTITUTIONAL ADVANCEMENT (IA)?

The noted "father of advancement," A. Westley Rowland (1986), defined institutional advancement as "develop[ing] understanding and support from all its constituencies in order to achieve its goals in securing such resources as students, faculty, and dollars" (p. xiii). We would further simplify the definition to "managing the institution's external relationships" so as to reinforce that advancement is not just about raising money and is not a short-term endeavor. Rather, it is about managing institutional-individual relationships that sometimes last a lifetime (e.g., child of an alumnus who grows up with the institution, attends, graduates, and remains an active alum until death), and certain interinstitutional relationships that can span an institution's entire existence (e.g., town-gown, professional/industrial societies, longtime employer of graduates).

It is important to note that IA is not simply "begging for money," as it is often cynically defined. Indeed, asking for support, financial and otherwise, must occur in order for an institution to be successful. However, this narrow misconception about both IA's purpose and the tasks required of its personnel too often keeps prospective partners on the outside. Arguably the profession itself is at least partially responsible for maintaining a veil of mystery when in fact the fundamentals of advancement work are basic human nature and can be learned by all.

While the mission of IA is essentially identical across all colleges and universities, significant differences certainly exist. For example, the importance of alumni and private foundations at a small liberal arts college may be supplanted by the corporate and government sectors at a regional comprehensive university. Beyond priority ordering of constituent groups, the largest difference will come from how institutional advancement is organized, controlled, and resourced, and how its specific goals are prioritized.

The most basic form of organization is what was commonly called the "three legs of the stool" or the three essential administrative function areas: development, communications, and alumni relations. More recently, the traditional back-office functions of advancement services (i.e., database management, gift processing, research) have emerged as a distinctive and separate "fourth leg."

As many variations of this organizational structure exist as there are distinctions in higher education. For example, an integrated advancement operation would find all four divisions under one chief advancement officer. Meanwhile, many institutions have development and alumni relations joined but keep the communications function separate. Still other institutions with independent alumni associations may structure all three functions as completely separate entities. Regardless of individual reporting lines and institutional traditions, the four functional areas are distinctive groups brought together only by a shared mission and their professional association—CASE.

The other important structural difference is centralized versus decentralized control. Small institutions have centralized "small shop" advancement operations that keep decision making and emphasis centrally controlled. This is a straightforward organizational structure that makes PA-IA cooperation rather simple. Meanwhile, many larger and more complex institutions have selected centralized functions and controls combined with a network of decentralized satellites at the various units/regions/colleges/campuses. This model delegates defined measures of control over constituents, message, and overall advancement activities to unit-level professionals. Under the best of circumstances this can be a very effective method of managing the institutional relationships at the level of common experience, provided that efficiencies are maximized through centralized administrative functions. The inverse scenario is that units are too autonomous, which results in duplication and lack of coordination, which at the very least means inefficiencies and at the worst mismanagement of institutional relationships.

Lastly, institutional advancement has developed its own vernacular, which is both unique to the profession and variable from institution to institution. A simple title of development officer on one campus may be referred to as a major gifts officer, associate director of development, or even leadership

gifts officer at another. The best suggestion for understanding the IA no-
menclature at a particular institution is to simply review each position title
with the chief advancement officer(s), whatever his or her title may be.

PA ROLES IN INSTITUTIONAL ADVANCEMENT

Acknowledging the responsibilities already mentioned, and other more specialized roles, where and when does the PA intersect with the advancement
world? The first instance is communications with internal and external
constituents. Presidential assistants handle phone calls, e-mails, letters, and
face-to-face visits with each and every one of an institution's constituents.
Whether the PA is substituting for the president or dealing with a constituent's issue directly, those interactions carry significant consequences—good
and bad—depending on how they are handled. For example, addressing
the concerns of an upset constituent (e.g., donor, alumnus, parent, legislator) who is not satisfied with taking the matter to a specific office is a regular
occurrence, and in most cases the constituents are not even satisfied with
a response from the appropriate vice president. Presidents certainly don't
have time to hear each one of these concerns. PAs are sometimes given
primary responsibility for all university communications.

The extent of contact that presidential assistants have with the governing
board and other volunteer leadership is typically unparalleled by anyone
except the president and advancement vice president. This means that PAs
spend a lot of time engaged in everything from mundane to meaningful
personal interactions with the institution's most important constituents.
Presidential assistants sometimes carry the title and responsibilities of
board secretary and are therefore, after the president, the chief liaison to
many of these constituents (see chapter 8).

What about the regular occasions, which are ripe for conscious attention
to the appropriate parts of the donor cycle (i.e., identification, cultivation, so-
licitation, and stewardship)? One may be engaged in each of these practically
on a daily basis, sometimes formally when meeting with existing or perspective donors, but most often through informal interactions. Some PAs even
carry their own portfolios of major gift donors for which they alone are solely
responsible. For example, when Michael McGreevey served as presidential
assistant at Ithaca College he also served on the leadership team for the college's capital campaign, managing both prospective donors and volunteers.

Advancement-oriented interactions are not just limited to alumni or existing donors as many external relationships are critical for achieving short- and long-term success. As such, some PAs are charged with securing resources for their institutions from specific sources. For example, Jeffrey Johnson, formerly at the University of Puget Sound, had foundation relations as a part of his everyday job responsibilities. Similarly, while serving as a PA, Marcus Lingenfelter was expected to secure funding from state and federal sources as a matter of course.

Noticeably intertwined in all of this is the engagement of alumni—the enduring constituency of every institution. PAs may have meaningful interactions with alumni frequently, and they need to be documented. That's right, presidential assistants write contact reports too, certainly not as often or comprehensive as a director of advancement services would like, but they represent a very important mechanism for ensuring that the substance of those interactions is documented.

What about image quality control? Since the institutional and presidential images are interconnected—whether we like it or not—managing and ensuring quality are chief among the concerns of presidential assistants. If the president speaks at a special event that has not been well orchestrated, then the public will associate the bad event with the president and not with the entity that hosted the event. A presidential assistant can use an advancement lens to view and critique each and every event with which the president is involved.

PA-IA PARTNERSHIP: BENEFITS AND CHALLENGES

A trusting and productive working relationship between the Office of the President and IA is critical for the success of any academic presidency. The importance of securing external financial resources, properly articulating the president's message, and nurturing a knowledgeable and committed corps of supporters cannot be overstated in the current climate of higher education. The institutional leader is the primary actor in this multifaceted endeavor, which thus becomes a top priority for the PA.

An interoffice partnership can be as informal as regularly scheduled update meetings to as formal as creating an administrative position dedicated to ensuring synergies. That is the route the University of Rochester recently took with creation of the special assistant to the vice president for advancement and presidential liaison. This new position illustrates the needs and significant benefits to a strong interoffice partnership, such as:

- Better information flow between president and IA
- More efficient and effective use of the president's time with IA activities
- Better management of the president's prospects
- Better execution of the president's events and IA activities

While not every institution can afford to staff at this level, the benefits can still be achieved through cooperation and understanding between the chief advancement officer and the PA. Cooperation to the point, as advocated earlier, that the PA be considered an adjunct member of the IA team is most desirable. This is a way to ensure proper interoffice coordination as well as to augment the IA staff complement, therefore serving the institution.

This relationship is not without potential challenges or even pitfalls. This explanation is not meant to dissuade, but rather to inform so as to ensure success. These challenges are also not in any way unique to IA, but rather common to PAs' interactions with most administrative units. It is not uncommon to find vice presidents or other staff who jealously guard their territory, or even underperforming units that may try to conceal information. It would be best for the PA to navigate these difficult situations by ensuring that the president is fully informed and is in a position to provide complete backing to achieve the desired objectives.

IA PROFESSIONAL DEVELOPMENT

As the doctoral dissertation "Career Paths of Presidential Assistants" (Miles, 2000) illustrates, defining a clear pathway to the role of PA is difficult at best. Lingenfelter's pathway to becoming a PA was through advancement, as was that of the recent NAPAHE chair Beth Brooks, who served as a major gifts officer prior to becoming PA at The Colorado College. However, the majority of PAs still desire some form of professional development in the realm of institutional advancement. This is easily accomplished through thoughtful and comprehensive training in three venues: (1) the PA's home institution, (2) NAPAHE, and (3) CASE. (Note: there are other professional development programs for higher education advancement at selected institutions, but CASE is the most common and accessible source of training in the advancement profession.)

Training for a PA should begin with the simple notion that not all advancement comprises asking for money. There are a number of critical administrative functions in IA that never require a person to sit face-to-face with a prospective donor and make the "ask." For example, donor relations/stewardship is already a common function performed by most PAs each and every time they work with their governing board members. Furthermore, new members of the advancement profession, once properly acclimated, quickly find that reticence to make the ask is replaced by excitement and joy. This would certainly be the case for PAs as well.

To conclude, advancement is a critical element of every modern American college and university. It is an administrative function to which all presidents, regardless of their experience with or proclivities toward, must dutifully attend. Therefore, a presidential assistant who is both knowledgeable of and intimately involved with this area can both better serve the president and expand his or her own administrative portfolio. Moreover, an advancement-savvy PA can ensure effective and efficient interoffice operations, leading to a more successful presidential term.

REFERENCES

Miles, B. S. (2000). Career paths of presidential assistants in higher education. Doctoral dissertation, Columbia University.

Rowland, A. W. (1986). *Handbook of institutional advancement* (2nd ed.). San Francisco: Jossey-Bass.

7

EXECUTIVE SPEECHWRITING AND OTHER COMMUNICATIONS

Richard P. Haven and Kevin Boatright[1]

Communication is an important part of effective executive leadership. This is especially true at a college or university, where the president is expected to be a highly visible, highly literate advocate for the institution. As a public speaker or writer, the president can influence the perceptions and actions of alumni, faculty, students, parents, legislators, and the public enormously— for good or ill.

Because communication is so important—and can, in fact, be seen as the highest form of symbolic leadership—it's not unusual for the presidential assistant to be expected to provide speechwriting support. What is unusual is for the assistant to have much experience writing texts (speeches, letters, reports, etc.) for someone else to present. Most have not done it before and few have any idea how to begin. Some even view it as improper.

Therefore, speechwriting is an important skill for presidential assistants to develop and practice. There are few other assignments that can have as much impact, or which will endear the presidential assistant to the president more—if done well. The rewards can be considerable, in terms of one's relationship with the president and contribution to the institution (or need for a creative outlet).

No one is born a speechwriter. Most presidential assistants need to un-learn their existing writing styles in order to write speeches that are faithful to the speaker's voice and viewpoint. Writing and presenting papers for academic conferences, for example, is usually of little value when one's goal is a text that, in Peggy Noonan's words, is "part theater and part political declaration." She adds that "a speech is poetry: cadence, rhythm, imagery, sweep!" (1990, p. 68). Most academic writing does not fit that description.

Few presidents have time to research and write speeches or op-ed articles. The assistant can focus on the speech and tailor it to a specific audience. Just as important, the assistant can take care that next week's speech at a service club is consistent with the theme of this year's annual report and the thrust of last year's capital campaign.

Skills developed and practiced as a speechwriter can be adapted to all the other forms of presidential communication: correspondence, a column for the alumni magazine, resolutions and commendations, reports to the board, fund-raising letters, and brief statements for news releases. If one can write with a certain amount of dramatic flair—enough to bring the text to life while being faithful to the speaker—being the president's speechwriter is an opportunity for greater access, increased influence, a creative challenge, and even some fun.

WORKING WITH YOUR SPEAKER

The relationship between the speechwriter and speechmaker is critical. The speechwriter needs full access to the speechmaker, and must understand the speechmaker enough to adapt to his or her beliefs, values, style, and preferences. This access includes informal conversations that permit the speechwriter to discuss a variety of topics with the president. It also includes participation in staff meetings, the availability of vice presidents for consultation, and the ability to research all information sources (including personnel files).

The speechwriter must develop an in-depth knowledge of the campus that includes a working understanding of the critical issues of the moment as well as the institution's past successes and failures. A comprehensive historical perspective aids the speechwriter—and thus the president—in addressing issues and avoiding mistakes. Since many presidents' institutional memory may be short, the assistant can help a president understand the traditions and practices of the past and thus better navigate dangerous waters.

The speechwriter needs to learn the speaker's delivery preferences, such as whether the president prefers extemporaneous, manuscript, memory, or a combination of these modes of speaking. The speechwriter also needs to learn the president's preferences regarding speech notes (e.g., full manuscript, partial manuscript, bullet points, brief note cards).

One approach is not necessarily better than another. What works for the president is what is important. However, the impromptu mode (little or no preparation or notes) is not recommended. The opportunity for error is great, and audiences generally notice even small mistakes. Errors harm the effectiveness of a speech as well as the credibility of the speechmaker.

To be successful, the speechwriter has to develop a good chemistry with the speaker and learn to write in the president's voice. In a sense, the speechwriter and the president need to develop friendship, mutual respect, and a sense of coauthorship regarding the speech. Once they begin to function as a team, both parties will be more successful.

One of the most difficult adjustments for any speechwriter is to suspend his or her own beliefs and judgments and write from the basis of the president's point of view. Ideally, the speechwriter and president are in agreement, but this may not always be the case. Finally, the speechwriter needs to project the speechmaker's personality so that the audience not only hears a coherent and interesting message but also comes away with a greater knowledge of, fondness for, and respect for the president.

However, others in the organization may not appreciate the speechwriter's role. Some will try to take advantage of the speechwriter's access to the president, while others will attempt to undercut his or her involvement in critical discussions and the decision-making process. The speechwriter needs to establish a good working relationship with all the people who have a stake in the president's decision-making process. While the speechwriter may not have much institutional power, he or she can have significant influence. Using that influence wisely is a key to success.

SPEECHWRITING IS NOT PLAGIARISM

Politicians have used speechwriters effectively for decades. For college and university presidents, however, the notion of using a speechwriter may suggest plagiarism or academic fraud. Using a speechwriter is not unethical. Intellectually, a speech is not the same as a dissertation. A president's speech is a corporate communication, not just a personal one. It is delivered on behalf of the whole institution and reflects institutional objectives. This is true even when the president is addressing an issue not directly related to the campus.

The true ethical issues involving a speech or any other form of communication have to do with proper attribution. Has the speechwriter identified the source of quoted material? Is the content accurate and verifiable? Does it correctly reflect the speaker's views and those of the institution? Failure to deal with these questions properly can lead to serious trouble for the speaker, the speechwriter, and the institution.

Ethically, it is also important that the speechwriter not take undue personal credit for the text. A speechwriter can acknowledge—if asked—that he or she "assisted" the speaker. Nothing more. Few speeches are delivered verbatim. Decisions made by the speaker determine the final form of the speech, which becomes the property of the speaker as it is being delivered. The speechwriter should take pride in work done for the president, but the president is the one who should get the credit for the ideas, the language, and the presentation.

PREPARATION OF A SPEECH

A number of factors need to be considered when preparing a speech for the president. If the speechwriter has control of the president's schedule, ask whether the invitation merits the president's attention. A reduction in the president's speaking engagements may be in order, given his or her other duties, the nature of the event, the other speakers invited, or the sponsoring organization. For example, some student organizations will invite two or three administrators to give welcoming speeches. If a dean and the provost are already scheduled, it may be redundant for the president to speak as well.

Once a speech is scheduled, it's important to focus on the audience, occasion, event, sponsoring organization, and related issues. First and foremost, analyze the audience. Who is the primary audience (students, faculty, alumni, parents, community leaders, etc.)? The speech must focus on the primary audience. Second, are there secondary or multiple audiences (parents and students, faculty and alumni, etc.)?

Many speeches involve multiple audiences. The president needs to recognize all audience segments, being careful not to offend one while speaking to the other. In the case of a State of the University address, the president's primary audience may be the faculty and staff, but secondary audiences include members of the governing board, legislators, alumni, students, and community members. These secondary audiences may access the speech through the news media or by reading a copy on the web. One must consider how the message will play to the live audience as well as to later audiences. Awareness of multiple audiences may affect the kind of humor used, the examples cited, or the issues discussed.

In addition to analyzing the audience, the speechwriter needs to be aware of the occasion, the sponsoring organization, and any related issues that may affect the outcome of a particular speech. It is paramount that the president pay homage to any special occasion that is a part of the scheduled event. The occasion may be a national day of recognition (e.g., Secretaries Day, Veterans Day) or it may be a local day of recognition (e.g., student volunteerism, employee recognition). The speechwriter also needs to be aware of any secondary and inflammatory issues that may be germane to this speech. A speech to a local service club about the goals of the university cannot ignore the fact that the university's budget proposal is before the legislature and is generating some controversy.

The speechwriter needs adequate time to research the audience, event, and occasion. He or she also needs time to simply think, write, and rewrite as well as review drafts with the president. Lead time is a critical element: the more, the better. The president's appointments secretary should notify the speechwriter as soon as a speaking engagement is scheduled. Speechwriters generally need a shorter period of time to prepare welcoming speeches and a much longer period of time to prepare major policy addresses.

ORGANIZATION OF THE SPEECH

The fundamental organization of a speech has changed little over the centuries. It's how one handles the fundamentals that makes the difference between a memorable speech and one that is (best) forgotten.

The introduction gives the speaker a chance to break the ice, to set the tone, to recognize distinguished guests, and to remind the audience what the speech is all about. It's often a good place for some humor—especially if it sets the audience at ease concerning a difficult topic.

The main points come in the body of the speech. This is the meat of what the speaker has to say. "The most moving thing in a speech is always the logic," says Noonan. "A good case well argued and well said is inherently moving" (1998, p. 64). A century ago, speakers might go on for hours and touch on dozens of main points. Today, speeches are generally much shorter and two or three points are all the audience can digest at one sitting. It is better to speak well and memorably for fifteen to twenty minutes than to overstay one's welcome at the podium.

The conclusion provides an opportunity to tie up loose ends, repeat the main points, cement the connection between the topic and the audience, and provide a fitting climax. The speech should flow naturally toward its conclusion, so that the final sentence is as appropriate as the first. "You don't have to have a boffo ending," says Noonan. "And you should never try to make them cry. You should try to make them, or help them, think" (1998, p. 63). The speaker does not need a cymbal crash to leave the audience persuaded, inspired, and ready to act.

Sometimes, the most valuable part of the speech comes in the question-and-answer period that follows, or in the informal chats the president has while leaving the hall. The speechwriter cannot script these interchanges—but he or she can brief the president about what questions to expect and the temper of the audience.

A well-organized speech gives the impression of a well-organized president leading a well-organized institution. If that is the only impression the speech leaves—if that's all the audience remembers after it forgets what was said—the speech has been successful.

USING HUMOR EFFECTIVELY

One of the most powerful devices available to any speaker is humor. It attracts the audience's attention and increases its affection for the speaker. Humor also has the potential to make a speech memorable and more effective, but it can be very dangerous. If poorly delivered, culturally offensive, or overused, humor can harm the goodwill that exists between audience and speaker, sidetrack the audience from the more important message, or require the speaker to apologize later.

While there are dangers to using humor, it should be at least considered for most speeches. The benefits can outweigh the dangers. In general, humor involving wordplay (puns) should be avoided. It can be funny but typically does not convey an image befitting a president. Irony, on the other hand, may be very appropriate. When one deals with budgets, alumni, parking, faculty members, and students on a regular basis, a little irony or sarcasm may not only be appropriate but cathartic.

The safest type of humor is self-deprecating humor. It's generally safe to make fun of oneself. Any time the president can relate a humorous story based on his or her childhood or a more recent experience, that story usually will be well received.

The humorous stories of others can also be useful, especially if the subject is a powerful or highly respected person. It is usually okay to poke a little fun at politicians, unless the president is addressing a group of politicians (then be sure it's about the other political party). Telling a story that derives its humor from one's gender, race, ethnic group, or sexual orientation is inviting disaster.

One must also consider the delivery of humor. Telling a joke well requires two concurrent factors: accuracy and timing. A good joke teller is someone who can remember the joke correctly (especially the punch line) and can deliver it in a way that sets up the punch line for maximum effectiveness.

In the end, the speechwriter and the president must decide whether humor should be used and what kind of humor works for each situation. Not all presidents are comfortable telling jokes or humorous stories. If that is the case, the speechwriter may live a humorless existence! On the other hand, most presidents like to incorporate some humor into their speeches. Some will be superb storytellers, while others may not be quite as comfortable. The speechwriter may discover that a well-placed quote here or there will suffice.

Humor is powerful. If used wisely and sparingly, the president's speeches will be enhanced.

MAKING THE SPEECH

If the president came up through the faculty ranks, he or she may need to stop giving an academic paper and start making a speech. Both the speechwriter and the president need to think of public address as a performance rather than a form of punishment for the audience. For the speechwriter, that means inserting short or even partial sentences, as well as dramatic pauses, repeated expressions, underlined words and phrases, rhetorical questions, and other devices that make the speech easier for the speaker to express and easier for the listeners to comprehend. It also requires consciously avoiding awkward passages that can twist the most nimble tongue.

A president need not be a William Jennings Bryan or a Barack Obama in order to be effective. Great speeches can be made by less-than-great speakers. Inexperienced public speakers will have to work at it, however. Encourage rehearsal, private critiques, videotape review, and personal coaching (as necessary). Ideally, the coaching and critique would be done by a third party. Thin-skinned presidents may resent criticism of their delivery technique. It's best if they hear that from someone other than the presidential assistant.

It is smart to attend as many of the president's speaking engagements as possible and to listen to how he or she speaks. Noting what was changed from the final draft, being sensitive to inflections, and how words are emphasized or de-emphasized can lead to an even better job the next time.

SOME SPEECHES FAIL

Sometimes, no matter how carefully a text is researched and written or no matter how well the president delivers it, a speech can fail. It turned out to be the wrong audience, the wrong day, or the wrong remarks, and the result is a resounding thud. Now what?

First, do not be personally offended by the audience reaction. If the speechwriter and the president both did their best, neither can be blamed for the outcome. If the president is speaking in a town where a major plant closing was announced that morning, it's likely no one in the audience is thinking about the speech. Given some warning, however, it would be an opportunity for the president to preface the prepared remarks with a sincere expression of sympathy and perhaps an offer of assistance. This would help the audience focus on what's about to be said.

Even when a speech seems like a failure, one can make the best of it. The president can keep smiling (literally) and try to capitalize on questions from the audience. The Q&A session often lasts longer than the actual speech, so it gives a perceptive speaker a second chance to make key points, to make a lasting impression, and to achieve the initial purpose.

For the presidential assistant, it may be that a failed speech can be revised and tried again on a different date in a different place with a different audience. A speech should not be thrown away if all it needs is some minor changes and a new set of circumstances. It is also possible that the speech can be recycled as a letter from the president in a staff or alumni publication, or recast entirely as an op-ed article in a newspaper or magazine.

USING MULTIMEDIA PRESENTATION SOFTWARE EFFECTIVELY

Multimedia presentation software (such as PowerPoint) has become the rage in public speaking. It can enhance a speech and improve the effectiveness of the speaker. However, it can also be overused or used in an inappropriate fashion.

Generally, it is wise to avoid multimedia enhancement when giving short speeches such as welcomes, introductions, dedications, or tributes. Longer speeches, such as a State of the University address, a ponderous report to the board, or a presentation to alumni may be enhanced by using multimedia presentation software. Programs such as PowerPoint enable the speaker to enhance the visual appeal of the presentation and to keep audiences interested longer. The slides can introduce humor, provide a virtual tour of new facilities, reinforce values (diversity, excellence, caring environment), and recognize faculty and staff members who have achieved noteworthy awards. People always appreciate seeing their picture on the big screen when they are identified by the president.

Multimedia programs can be used for more than just slides, of course. With the right equipment, a speaker can show video clips of sports teams in action, recitals, plays, faculty interaction with students, commencement, and much more. Clips can be built into the presentation so that the speaker can move from slide to video and back again seamlessly. Animation also enables the speaker to introduce main points or new topics more effectively.

Along with the usual equipment needs (laptop computer, data/video projector, screen, amplifiers/speakers, proper lighting) it may be useful to consider other devices to enhance the presentation. An "air mouse" frees the speaker to move around, and a portable audio microphone is highly recommended to enhance sound quality and volume. The technology keeps changing, so a speechwriter must stay current with advances in equipment and software.

The speechwriter, or another qualified person, should assist the president in the use of presentation software. The president needs to interact with the audience before and after the speech. Having an assistant on hand will free the president for such interaction. It is imperative that whoever assists the president rehearse the presentation with him or her, and work out any bugs in advance.

In the case of major address like the State of the University, consider using video, PowerPoint slides, and even projecting the president's image on a large screen while he or she speaks. The proper use of these enhancements will help make a long speech more interesting and more memorable. The presidential assistant, of course, can function much like a television director changing the images on the screen from video to slides to live camera as demanded by the speech.

The presidential assistant will also need to learn how to develop multimedia slides. Learning to use a program is fairly simple, and it can be an enjoyable and creative activity. Programs such as PowerPoint offer shortcut design features that enable the speechwriter to put together a slide show in a relatively short period of time.

When preparing lengthy speeches, one might consider forming a design team to assist. The speechwriter may wish to involve the director of the auditorium where the speech will occur, the director of news services, a graphic design specialist who can create the slides, and a staff member with experience in video and sound editing. Using a design team enables the speechwriter to develop a much more sophisticated and impressive presentation.

RESOURCES FOR THE SPEECHWRITER

Effective speechwriters have access to resources that assist them in the preparation of interesting, accurate, and inspirational speeches. Reading and listening to speeches by other university presidents or by famous people (e.g., Franklin Roosevelt, John F. Kennedy, Ronald Reagan, Martin Luther King Jr.) will help the assistant develop a better understanding of the techniques that make a speech memorable and different from other forms of communication.

The speechwriter also needs to build a personal, unique speechwriter's library. This library should include books, trade publications, Internet sites, institutional documents, and news sources. It's helpful to obtain books of quotations, sayings, speeches, and poetry. An example is Diane Ravitch's *The American Reader* (1990), which includes speeches, poetry, songs, and other documents from American history. Ideally, this library will include useful works of history, biography, and autobiography.

Trade publications, such as the *Speechwriter's Newsletter* (published by Lawrence Ragan Communications), provide a wealth of up-to-date material that can be used to enhance a speech. The speechwriter may also wish to bookmark Internet sites that provide useful information or tips on speechwriting. These sites include NAPAHE (www.napahe.org), Gifts of Speech (women's speeches from around the world; gos.sbc.edu), Speeches.com (a variety of topics regarding speechwriting; speeches.com), and the History Channel (www.historychannel.com).

One of the best sources of information for a president's speeches is the campus itself. Important documents, publications, and brochures produced by the institution (including a campus history) contain facts, figures, and other useful information for fleshing out remarks. News sources can aid the speechwriter in obtaining information, including the higher education associations, CNN, *USA Today*, and other national news organizations. Their websites and databases can be useful in verifying or locating needed information. Finally, the local press and the reporters one deals with on a regular basis, along with other contacts on the campus and in the community, can verify information and thus help ensure the accuracy of the speech.

FINAL THOUGHTS

Knowing how to write speeches for a president is half the task. The other half is having something important to say, and being courageous enough to say it with eloquence and integrity. Some long for the days when college and university presidents were prominent speakers on major topics—"public intellectuals" in the best sense of the word. For many of today's presidents—given the demands on their time and the limitations of their situations—that is not possible, even with an excellent assistant.

Still, it is a goal to strive toward if the president has the vision and the desire to transcend the campus and offer insights into a range of regional, national, or global issues. Rita Bornstein, president emerita of Rollins College, posed the challenge this way:

> The prestige of the college presidency assures an audience for a president's ideas, providing a bully pulpit unequaled in most realms of public life. Despite this privileged access to the public, today's college and university presidents are perceived as silent and lacking in leadership on important public policy issues. Indeed, it is the rare president who has the time, expertise, and independence to establish a leadership role in national affairs. . . . On national and local issues, presidents can help raise the level of discourse above factional loyalties, contribute a broad historical perspective, identify ethical problems, provide acceptable alternatives for consideration, and stake out a position. (Bornstein, 1995, p. 56)

If a president aspires to become that "rare president" Bornstein is describing, he or she will need a gifted speechwriter who can help frame ideas into words.

"Politicians want to look good so they can get things done," writes Noonan. "[Corporate] CEOs want to get things done so they can look good." A university president is perhaps both politician and corporate CEO. For presidential assistants who want to be good speechwriters, it's important to remember that and to heed Noonan's final words of advice: "For corporate speechwriters it means keeping an undeviating eye on the boss's agenda and making sure the speech advances it" (1998, p. 133).

NOTE

1. With assistance from Lorrie Kyle, executive assistant to the president, Rollins College.

REFERENCES

Bornstein, R. (1995). Back in the spotlight: The college president as public intellectual. *Educational Record*, 76(4).

Noonan, P. (1990). *What I saw at the revolution: A political life in the Reagan era.* New York: Random House.

Noonan, P. (1998). *Simply speaking: How to communicate your ideas with style, substance, and clarity.* New York: Regan Books.

Ravitch, D. (1990). *The American reader: Words that moved a nation.* New York: HarperCollins.

8

ONCE UPON A MOTION: A BOARD SECRETARY'S TALE

Nancy Kelly

On many college and university campuses, the executive assistant to the president serves as secretary to the board of trustees. Of the presidential assistants responding to the NAPAHE survey, fully one-quarter hold both or similar titles, and over one-third, 36 percent, report "interaction with the governing board" to be a major activity. With the exception of the president, who often also is a trustee, the board secretary has the closest and most sustained relationship to the board as a whole, to individual trustees, and to the chair of the board. This uniquely privileged view of higher education's chief stewards increases the intellectual, logistical, and, at times, emotional gymnastics required to do both jobs well.

The day-to-day work life of an assistant to the president can be about triage, about a steady stream of small or large emergencies that, once resolved, keep things running smoothly. The day-to-day work life of the secretary to the board of trustees is very different. Most of the activity is planned and takes place systematically before, during, and after board meetings. The secretary's schedule can consist of stretches of quietude followed by bursts of complex, varied activity, and the planning and communication that happens during those peaceful interludes can determine the success of the board's meetings and the degree of board members' engagement with the institution. The secretary's position has great flexibility and provides its incumbent many opportunities to serve the college or university in important ways.

Beyond ensuring the completeness and accuracy of board minutes and maintaining a permanent and secure record of board actions, there are few absolutes in the secretary's role. It is extremely shortsighted, however, to assume that precise minutes define or limit the secretary's role. "Describe the secretary as accountable for the accuracy of board documents," John Carver and Miriam Mayhew Carver write with pithy accuracy of their own in *Reinventing Your Board: A Step-by-Step Guide to Implementing Policy Governance* (1997). The Carvers then go on, with equally pithy dismissiveness, to posit, "This is probably all that needs to be said about this position" (p. 169). Not so.

Concise and consistent communication is surely the foundation of building a solid relationship with the board. However, each board is different in its expectations. Some boards want to see it all—a calendar of campus events, working documents, student newspaper, and external publications such as the *Chronicle of Higher Education*. Some want one-page executive summaries and one-page meeting agendas. Figuring out the balance is not daunting; board members generally are not shy about making their preferences known. As a working rule, it may be useful to think about "bundling" correspondence so that general-interest, "FYI" pieces are sent with meeting materials and that mailings between meetings are minimized. Sending a general update between meetings is useful, but filling board members' mailboxes with every college publication is usually a nuisance to them and an expense for the institution.

Increasingly, many institutions have found e-mail a valuable tool for communicating with the board, although it is best reserved for general information and nonconfidential correspondence. The Hampshire College office of college communications, for example, sends weekly summaries of all press releases and news stories (with URL links) to board members via e-mail, a practice extremely popular with board members. It is apparent that the web will assume increasing importance in communicating with trustees, and will permit the news junkies on the board on-demand access to lengthy documents.

The substance of communication, of course, is of greater importance than the mechanics. Accuracy, completeness, and brevity are a given, but so, too, is awareness of board members' areas of individual interest. It is valuable to tailor mailings to keep trustees informed about their favorite special topics.

What board members say may be even more crucial. It is common courtesy to listen attentively, of course, but it is also essential to the secretary's job and to the board's well-being. At the most basic level, listening and responding appropriately to a trustee signals that he or she is a respected member of the board whose contributions are valued. Trustees, moreover, will tell things to the secretary that they will not say directly to the president either because of scheduling difficulties, or because of comfort levels, or because they want the secretary to deliver the message. As go-between in these instances, the secretary should report objectively but completely, and encourage the trustee to speak directly with the president.

Board members deserve responses. "Hearing back" is among the most important parts of communication, and it applies in all areas of board relations: answering routine requests promptly; following up on board actions and informing the board of the follow-up in a timely fashion; and letting board members know the use to which their advice has been put. Nothing makes a trustee's enthusiasm flag faster than making a suggestion to an administrator that falls in the black hole or answering a question from a board committee that garners no reply. If, for example, the nominating committee or committee on trustee membership asks board members for suggestions regarding potential trustees, it is up to the secretary to ensure that those suggestions are acknowledged. The art of the secretary's job is perhaps no more evident than when he or she follows up on a suggestion that languishes on a colleague's desk or in a board committee. Of course honesty is the best policy, provided it is tempered with tact and appreciation.

On independent college campuses in particular, administrative colleagues, faculty, and students can regard the board as remote and out of touch, thus leading to the occasional lag time in a colleague responding to a board member's request. The secretary can work with the president and the board to reduce, but perhaps not eliminate completely, this perception by drafting statements from the chair that give the campus constituencies a summary of what took place at board meetings, by making available short biographies of the trustees, and by promoting occasions for groups to meet informally. That the board should be perceived on campus as somewhat remote is not a bad thing; it is, in fact, reality. Trustees are not resident members of the campus community, are not involved in the day-to-day management of the institution, and are most valuable to the college when they can provide informed but impartial guidance.

The discourse that takes place during board and board committee meetings is of central importance. It is the secretary's role to ensure that trustees' participation is informed by the meeting materials. Adequate time must be provided—at least one week, although two is better—for board members to read meeting materials carefully and thoroughly. Materials generally include a detailed schedule and agenda, minutes of the previous meeting and minutes of board committee meetings, internal reports, and position papers relevant to the agenda. The latter are important so that less administrative reporting need take place during meetings. For the same reason, minutes should clearly show votes, resolutions, and other board actions. The more board members can participate in the debate, the higher their level of engagement. Trustees are volunteers; therefore, the time they allot to board business is limited and precious. The clarity and cogency of materials prepared for the board should reflect the institution's understanding of this valuable commodity. Such understanding is a tacit means of expressing appreciation for the work trustees undertake on behalf of the college. Given the work they do, board members cannot be thanked too often or in too many ways.

Preparing for board meetings is similar to preparing a course. A vast amount of material needs to be reviewed, sorted, and condensed in advance. Much like a syllabus, board meeting materials should include readings, schedule (agenda), and assignments (proposed actions and resolutions). The analogy can be stretched even further: the board meeting can take on aspects of a team-taught class, in which there are presentations by colleagues, then general discussion. To the extent that the secretary and his or her colleagues facilitate board discussion with relevant materials, background, analyses, and recommendations, the classroom analogy is apt. Once the board begins its work of institutional stewardship, however, the parallels to the classroom end. Trustees exist to establish and oversee institutional policy. In other words, they think and critique, judge and decide. They should be given the means to take on these tasks, and then let go to work.

Keeping trustees engaged with the college is the first order of business, and all communication should endeavor to keep that engagement fresh and attentive. Reports, e-mails, and agendas, essential as they are to the conduct of board business, do not suffice as the sole means of institutional communication with the board. Most trustees care deeply about teaching and learning, research and scholarship, the arts and sports. It goes without saying that telling trustees about what goes on in the classroom or the dance studio or the hockey rink is less compelling than showing them. Direct communication with students, faculty, and staff gives trustees an opportunity to experience the fruits of their hard work.

On a number of campuses, faculty and student representatives sit with the board either as observers or full voting members of the board. It is unrealistic to assume that any one faculty member or student can alone represent the richness of what takes place on campus. Creating opportunities for trustees to meet informally with students and faculty helps board members feel more connected to the college, more informed (without "administrative filter") about current campus trends and events, and, most importantly, affirms them as trustees. Simply inviting board members to share a meal with students in the dining hall, followed by dessert with faculty, has proven a popular exercise with many board members.

Trustees also welcome time to converse with fellow trustees absent the press of business or the presence of intrusive staff. Annual or biennial retreats address this need. So too do social occasions built into the schedule of board meetings, for example, a dinner before or after the meeting takes place. Such dinners are good opportunities for board members to bond with each other and to form a more cohesive whole. The same level of care and attention to detail that is part of preparing for board meetings should also be given to ancillary events, which are another means of thanking trustees for their stewardship and letting them know the college is grateful for their help.

Serving as secretary to the board of trustees draws on the same skills of tact, discretion, and judgment required of the presidential assistant, and the fact that the ebb and flow of the two jobs are different makes it possible for the same person to hold both positions simultaneously.

Combining the roles of board secretary and executive assistant strengthens the working bond between the president and his or her assistant. The secretary advises the president on both those strategic issues and external concerns the board should consider as well as the best strategies for working with the board. Like any volunteer organization, a board of trustees consists of individuals of diverse backgrounds who share an interest. Some boards, however, can be less diverse in outlook and point of view than others, and, under such circumstances, the secretary working for and with the president has a tacit responsibility to break through the logjam in thinking that can take place when board members are too like-minded.

The obvious example, of course, is a board that is made up in the main or exclusively by graduates of the college. While the affection and the loyalty alumni board members hold for the institution is abiding, so too can be their perception of the institution, fixed somewhere during the years they called the campus home. A little nostalgia is a good thing, but keeping trustees current is even better, and it is essential to their role as policymakers. This is not a job the president or the secretary can do alone; however, given the close relationship the secretary has with both the president and the board, the secretary is ideally situated to seek out and implement ways to broaden board members' understanding of the college in its present state.

There is one area, though, where the executive assistant/secretary to the board of trustees should proceed with extreme caution. It is essential for the executive assistant/secretary to safeguard against ever confusing reporting lines. No matter how involved with board business, or how frequently in touch with board members, the executive assistant/board secretary reports formally, and ultimately, to the president. Temptations, fed by motivations benign or Machiavellian, to blur the lines or even to cross over them can be powerful: the trustee who asks "what you *really* think"; the committee chair who politely insists on reviewing a draft report the president has yet to review; the board chair who insists on speaking with the secretary rather than the president. At worst, such scenarios signal dark days ahead for the relationship between the board and the president and, needless to say, between the president and the executive assistant.

Fortunately, the worst case is seldom the reality, and is more likely the result of thoughtless or hurried behavior of the trustee, a volunteer with many commitments other than the institution. So, what to do? Responding to a trustee who wants "to know what you *really* think" depends on institutional culture. On many campuses, the executive assistant/board secretary is considered a member of the senior administration, and his or her contributions to policy discussion are expected and valued. In such circumstances, it may be appropriate to speak up. If, on the other hand, a trustee is asking the executive assistant/board secretary to second-guess or critique a presidential decision, one might diplomatically offer to have the president explain the background or context of said decision and save the gloss for the president's ears.

In the same spirit, a board secretary should not unilaterally share draft documents. In the first place, by their nature they are incomplete, and therefore potentially misleading. In addition, once a document is out, it is impossible to pull it back. Just because boards meet periodically, it is foolish to assume trustees do not talk among themselves in between meetings. They do, and moreover they share information, both behaviors to be encouraged as they show commitment to the institution. But activity based on incomplete or inaccurate information is a waste of the trustee's valuable time. Far better to provide regular updates to trustees that show where a particular issue is within the campus system—under discussion by the faculty, under study in the president's cabinet, under review by legal counsel. In possession of such information, the board member can feel assured that by the time the issue reaches a board committee, questions of fact have been asked and answered and questions of liability, if applicable, have also been considered and that the document is "clean" and ready for a policy review by the board.

There are other areas where the secretary must tread lightly, but they are seldom hidden. The simplest guideline is to keep in mind that trustees are not colleagues; no matter how closely staff members work with the board, or how long trustees and staff serve the same institution, the institutional commitment they share does not put them on equal footing. It does create, though, a common ground whereupon the secretary witnesses and records decisions that shape the future of higher education. It is a uniquely privileged position.

In conclusion, here are a few practical measures for organizing board meetings and for maintaining good relations with trustees:

- Schedule meetings as far in advance as possible—one year, if this is doable. A year's schedule is the norm for meetings of the full board; however, many trustees also find a year's calendar of committee meetings helpful. Advance notice makes it possible for the board member to build the college's business into his or her own schedule. More difficult to achieve, but just as useful, is to develop agendas well in advance, too. Staff to board committees should encourage committee chairs to develop the topics that will occupy the committee for its yearly meetings. Most trustees are appreciative if these agendas are shared with the entire board so that each board member feels "in the know." If following through on this suggestion requires delicate negotiations with colleagues who staff board committees or if it requires browbeating those colleagues, so be it.

- Begin and end meetings on time. Although such a basic principle is a given, the level of irritation felt by some trustees at meetings that do not run as scheduled can be acute, and the secretary, justly or not, will feel the brunt of it. It is a measure of respect for the gift of board members' time to husband it wisely and to maintain the published schedule.

- Distribute meeting materials well in advance of board meetings. In addition to the minutes, agenda, and backup material necessary for board meetings, executive summaries of lengthy documents should also be part of the package. Even trustees who read every word of every document appreciate intelligent summaries of dense or arcane reports. They also appreciate summaries of board votes and resolutions to supplement the more detailed minutes of board meetings.

- A display of excess in the service of thanking board members for their hard work is no vice. Trustees assume a serious responsibility when they join the board and deserve every bit of appreciation the college can offer them. Recognizing board members' service with thanks is mandatory, of course, but so too is reminding them of the reasons they do what they do. It is important to keep board members informed of faculty research and students' academic achievements; to find ways to let them know how board policies and decisions affect campus life; and to ensure their physical and gustatory comfort upon visits to campus. Most trustees are not interested in the college's resources being diverted to their care and feeding, however, so the challenge to the secretary is to accomplish all this while eschewing excess and, especially, the appearance of waste.

The secretary, of course, does none of this alone, and helping to strengthen the bonds between other senior staff and the board benefits the board and the institution. The closest working relationship, though, remains between the president and the secretary/assistant. Each can do and say things that the other cannot, and the complementary nature of the two positions vis-à-vis the board can be the most effective tool in maintaining good relations with the trustees.

REFERENCE

Carver, J., & Carver, M. M. (1997). *Reinventing your board: A step-by-step guide to implementing policy governance.* San Francisco: Jossey-Bass.

9

THE NASTY STUFF IN A PA'S LIFE: HANDLING COMPLAINTS

Steven J. Givens[1]

There's a story of a presidential assistant who was describing his job to a friend. After he finished, the friend paused for a moment and then responded, "So you're like the guy at the end of the parade with the shovel. . . ."

Very often, that is exactly right. Presidential assistants (PAs) do a lot of cleaning up, and sometimes it is pretty messy. This chapter deals with one of the most common aspects of a PA's job—handling complaints and other problems. How PAs handle these situations—and the systems they have in place for networking, listening, delegating, responding, following up, and documenting them—will say much not only about how they do their jobs but also about the overall quality and responsiveness of their president and institution. The buck may stop at the president's desk, but there is usually a PA to deflect and deal with it before it gets there.

In any given year, PAs deal with a wide range of complaints, problems, and issues, including student housing, crimes by and against students, admissions decisions, student health and well-being, transcripts, financial aid, sexual assault, alcohol, billing and collection, parking, off-campus residences, security, employee dissatisfaction, Internet and e-mail crime and harassment, disability and access, complaints against coaches and professors, Greek life, noise complaints from neighbors, study abroad fees, facility rentals, to name just a few.

Needless to say, most PAs are not in charge of any of these issues. But when an issue hits the president's office, it may become the PA's responsibility. Dealing with complaints and handling conflicts is a key aspect of a PA's job and very well could or should be a part of their job description. PAs need to be prepared and have a plan of action for the everyday complaints and issues that come across their desks as well as the "big and strange" issues that just seem to fall out of the sky.

This chapter sets out a list of ideas and suggestions for dealing with such complaints and also looks at the handling of special complaints and complainers. The chapter covers six specific topics:

1. Being prepared before the complaints come
2. Taking the complaint and handling difficult calls and visitors
3. Getting both sides of the story
4. Delegating to other administrators and knowing when and how to remove the issue from the president's office
5. Logging complaints and learning from history
6. Handling special and/or chronic complainers

BEING PREPARED AND GETTING STARTED

Within the president's office, it is important to establish protocols for handling and directing complaints. Decisions need to be made up front about where to direct the angry phone calls or visitors when they come. And they will come—sometimes in dribbles and sometimes in a flood. So it is first important to decide who within the office will be on the "frontline." These kinds of questions need to be answered:

- Will the calls or visitors be handled by the support person who receives them, or will he or she forward all calls to the PA?
- If they go to the PA, who takes such calls in the PA's absence?
- Has the support staff been trained in handling complaints?
- Will the president be apprised of every complaint that makes its way into the office? If so, when and how?

As in much of life and work, there are no right or wrong answers. Office protocols and procedures will come about as a consequence of the leadership and management styles of both the PA and the president. So it is crucial for PAs to communicate with their president and staff members and make sure everyone knows the ground rules and procedures.

Whether a PA is new in his or her position in the president's office or already has years of experience, a good place to begin training or retraining in complaint resolution is establishing or reinforcing a campus network of collaborators and problem solvers. For while PAs may be the people to whom other staffers look to solve problems, it is important to remember that rarely will they be the people who actually solve them. PAs will have their hands in the resolution, of course, but an effective PA is often only a facilitator and a communicator who gets the right people together and talking.

New PAs should spend their first week or two on the job setting up a network of campus collaborators and problem solvers. These are the people with whom they will have the most interaction on a day-to-day basis as problems and conflicts arise. This group will comprise many individuals, including people like the dean of students, chief of police or security, campus health director, general counsel and other lawyers, and the normal run of academic leaders such as deans, vice chancellors, and student affairs directors. PAs should and inevitably will continue to build this network throughout their careers by identifying those individuals who best represent the constituencies they are likely to be dealing with: students, faculty, staff, parents, alumni, trustees, neighbors, etc. These relationships will, in many ways, be the keys to their success as a PA.

Perhaps the biggest mistake that a PA can make is to envision himself or herself as a savior who swoops in to solve a problem when all else fails. That kind of problem solving can often create divisions within an organization and may cause the president's office and the president to be seen as a micromanaging entity that tells others what to do. Although there almost certainly will be times when the weight of a PA's position will be helpful and may need to be invoked, in almost all cases the best course of action will be to work with others and allow them to solve the problems. An invisible but effective and empowering PA is often the best PA.

A PA's job very often will be to listen carefully, take notes, and then find the correct person to whom to delegate. That is why it is so important that the required relationships are in place. A PA's collaborators need to know and trust him or her and feel that when they are speaking with the PA they are speaking to the president. PAs may have to earn the true respect of their colleagues over the years but must have the confidence and unwavering support of these people almost immediately in order to do their job well.

TAKING THE COMPLAINT

When the call comes or the visitor walks in, what should PAs do? The first thing, of course, is be a good listener. Anyone who comes to the president's office deserves to be listened to with respect and undivided attention. Because the PA does not yet know the real and whole truth of the circumstances, it is crucial that he or she listen to and interview this person just as a police officer takes a citizen complaint or a journalist interviews a witness.

Here are a few suggestions for handling interviews and asking good questions that will assist in getting to the heart of any matter. PAs should:

- Explain their role in a way that will help the person understand that a PA is the president's agent whose goal is to be helpful, provide the president with a briefing, or resolve the matter in the most efficient way possible.
- Remain objective, sympathetic, and calm, and save judgment for later.
- "Welcome" the complaint and let the person know his or her visit or call is appreciated.
- Set the person at ease and give him or her full attention by ignoring phones and computers. Remember that this may be a difficult situation for the individual. If the person is angry, this attentiveness will help disarm them.
- Begin by asking the person to simply tell the story of the complaint.
- Listen without interrupting and remember that sometimes people just want to "vent."
- Follow up by asking both fact-clarifying "short answer" questions and open-ended "essay" questions.
- Take good notes, unless to do so will unnerve the person. If notes are not taken during the meeting, a report should be written up immediately afterward.
- Cut to the quick. Do not be afraid to ask, "So what exactly do you want?" PAs should make sure they can identify the real problem, as well as the hoped-for solution.
- Acknowledge the problem and how the person feels about it, even though the full story may not yet be known.
- Promise that there will be follow-up by someone and that the person will receive a reply either from the PA or a designee within a few days. Never promise or even hazard a guess to the outcome to avoid raising false hopes.

Many people who call the president's office do so because they simply like to start at the top. Others feel that they haven't been heard by other offices at the college or university. In either case, a person should never leave a president's office or conclude a telephone conversation feeling the same way. A good practice is to promise all complainants three things: they will be listened to and taken seriously; their concerns will be acted upon in some way; they will receive a reply. Supplying good, accurate, and complete information is one of the quickest ways to resolve a conflict.

What a PA should never do is promise to resolve the person's problem in the way they want it resolved. Why? Because, so far, the PA has heard only one part of the story. A PA's ability to empathize with the person making the complaint, while not committing to that side of the story, is key to the PA's effectiveness as a problem solver. PAs should not make promises they may not be able to keep after learning the rest of the story. No matter how convincing the argument, no matter how horrendous the story sounds, PAs must remain objective until all of the facts are known.

GETTING BOTH SIDES

This is the part of the complaint process in which the PA becomes the detective. Following the interview with the complainant, it is helpful to consider and answer the following questions:

- What is the problem?
- What has already been tried?
- Who was mentioned?
- Who is responsible and/or involved?
- What can be done?

With the problem clearly defined, the PA can then set out to gather information. Contact should be made with any individuals mentioned by the person making the complaint, as well as with key collaborators on campus who are responsible for areas pertaining to the complaint. Very often these individuals will already know about this complaint and can quickly bring the PA up to speed on the issue. Nevertheless, PAs should listen to these sources just as carefully and objectively as they did the complainant. Occasionally, and depending upon an institution's policies, it may be helpful to request any written materials pertaining to the issue. A student's administrative file, for example, may contain the background documentation for a particular offense, including judicial proceedings and campus safety reports. These "primary" sources can be enormously helpful in getting a sense of exactly what took place and what steps the institution has taken since.

After a PA gets both sides of the story and shares it with his or her president (or not, depending upon procedures and the seriousness of the complaint), it may be time to do one of a number of things. It may be time for an executive decision by the PA or the president, or it may be time to delegate action to someone else.

DELEGATING RESPONSIBILITY AND RESPONSE

Some issues encountered by PAs may require a top-level decision by the president, perhaps in consultation with his or her top advisors and administrators. But other decisions are best handled by delegating the decision to the proper administrator.

Delegating is not simply passing the buck; it is empowering other individuals to do their jobs, allowing them to hear all sides of the story, make a decision, and devise a response. In addition, consistently deflecting problems from the president's office to the proper individuals will dissuade repeat complainers from "going to the top" all the time.

When PAs delegate an issue to someone else, it is important either to inform the complainant that the issue has been delegated or to ask the person to whom the issue has been delegated to respond on behalf of the president's office so the complainant recognizes that the president's office has been involved and responsive to the complaint. Likewise, if there is a written response to be made, the PA should always ask to be copied on the correspondence so that he or she knows how the issue has been resolved. In many ways, this is the best possible way to resolve a complaint.

Sometimes circumstances may dictate delegation and require that the PA let the complainant know of the president's interest and explain that delegating is not simply deflecting the concern back to the area that (perhaps) caused the problem in the first place. This approach illustrates the confidence the president has in his or her troops and shows that the PA is willing to monitor the situation and also usher the complainant through the process.

One question that arises for most PAs is when and under what circumstances should they delegate "up" to the president. In many ways, a PA's job is to deflect everyday problems so the president can concentrate on the important job of running the university or college, and many times minor complaints and problems can be handled without ever involving the president. Other times PAs will inform the president about a complaint and let him or her know how and when it is resolved.

But major issues or more serious complaints may require a president's involvement sooner and to a larger extent. Common sense should prevail here, with a general rule of thumb being: Would the president be embarrassed or hurt by not knowing this information? Would it be awkward to hear it from someone else besides the PA? If so, inform the president immediately.

Besides simply informing the president of an issue, there may be times when the president needs to be more fully involved. There are no hard-and-fast rules, once again, but the following circumstances might require direct intervention on the part of the president:

- Cases involving criminal activity by faculty, staff, or students
- Cases involving a president's direct reports or top administrators
- Cases involving an insistent individual who wishes only to speak to the president
- Cases that may end up in tomorrow's news

LOGGING COMPLAINTS

Although keeping records of complaints may seem obvious and logical, the value of history and the lessons to be learned from it cannot be emphasized enough. In the case of handling complaints in the president's office, it is important to create that history.

However a complaint ends up being handled, it is wise for PAs to record their actions or delegations and to send a copy of this report to their president and other individuals who are or who could be involved.

PAs should keep a file or notebook in their offices that contains notes from conversations and interviews dealing with complaints, including information about how the issue was resolved and any related correspondence. How long these files or notebooks should be kept on hand before they are archived will be a matter of individual protocols or preferences.

It is important to note that the North Central Association of Schools and Colleges (to comply with U.S. Department of Education regulations) now requires presidents' offices to keep a log of complaints received from students and a record of how the complaints were handled. In 1999, the NCA's Commission on Institutions of Higher Education issued a revised policy regarding maintenance of a log of student complaints that can be viewed by the evaluation team. (More information on this log can be found online at www.ncacihe.org/index.php under "File Third-Party Comments.")

In any case, having that history close at hand is good for numerous reasons, including dealing with a return complainer, dealing with a complaint that turns into a student judicial matter or a lawsuit, dealing with a similar complaint, or addressing core issues at the root of a pattern of complaints.

SPECIAL COMPLAINTS AND COMPLAINERS

Once in a while, PAs encounter those "special" individuals who demand an extraordinary amount of time and attention. These individuals might include people with mental health problems, but more often than not they are simply people with a heightened sense of their own importance and privilege (real or fictional), such as donors, parents, politicians, alumni, and other VIPs. Here are a few suggestions:

- Maintain clear and consistent communication lines with everyone involved, including the individual with the complaint. Make sure everyone at the university is "singing from the same page" with this complainer and that he or she gets the same response no matter where he or she goes.
- No matter how irrational the person is or how impossible it may seem to make him or her happy, it is important to engage complainants and make them feel that their issues are being heard.
- Know when to tell a complainant that the president's office is not the proper place for their complaint. Be able to explain the limitations of the president's office.
- Know when to "just say no" to unreasonable people.
- Ask the person how he or she would like to see the issue resolved. If the suggested solution is impossible or unclear, say so. The person may come to realize the futility of the complaint.
- If a complainant makes unreasonable demands (such as "so and so should be fired immediately!"), give a logical and reasonable response that may diffuse the situation. If necessary, put your response in writing and attempt to end the matter once and for all. Any further calls or discussion can then refer to this letter in which the PA stated the university's position.

- If someone demands to speak with the president or governing board, explain the role of the president and the governing board and suggest that the complaint be put in writing. Provide the person with the correct names and addresses. Then communicate with the president and governing board and suggest an appropriate response. Again, be sure that replies are consistent within the organization.
- Realize that some chronic complainers have real and justified complaints. Sometimes (and only under carefully considered circumstances) special complainers can be defused by engaging them more fully in the life of the university. PAs might ask these individuals to serve on a committee, write a report, or meet with them occasionally as "special consultants."

There is no doubt that a PA's role is challenging when it comes to handling complaints. But with the proper procedures and communication network in place and in use, a PA can master this responsibility. A PA who can consistently and effectively handle complaints is a true asset to the president's office and will gain respect throughout his or her institution as a "go-to" person who gets things done while empowering others.

NOTE

1. With assistance from Meredith Harper Bonham, executive assistant to the president, Hamilton College; Carol R. Braden, assistant to the president, The University of Texas Pan American; Lane Estes, vice president for administration, former assistant to the president, Birmingham–Southern College; Lori Neiswander, former executive assistant to the president, Case Western Reserve University; Marc Schaeffer, chief of staff, William Paterson University of New Jersey; Linda P. Shank, vice president for communication and strategic initiatives, former executive assistant to the president, Sweet Briar College.

10

PRESIDENTIAL ASSISTANTS AS SENIOR ADMINISTRATORS

Mark P. Curchack[1]

The Gilbert and Sullivan opera *The Mikado* has two main "official" characters, Ko-Ko, the Lord High Executioner, and Poo-Bah, Lord High Everything Else. Opinions will differ as to who plays the first role on most campuses. Might the presidential assistant be the Lord High Everything Else? Clearly, PAs wind up taking care of "everything else," as John Cummins's chapter in this volume abundantly shows. In this chapter, I wish to consider how "high" a lord a PA might be. Are there circumstances in which PAs are, or function as, senior administrators, leading the campus from outside the shadow of the president, and what are those conditions?

The role of presidential assistant, still relatively new in the panoply of higher educational titles, is, consequently, highly flexible. As documented in this volume, a wide variety of functions are performed by presidential assistants. These may be assigned all at once, or be added (rarely subtracted) during a presidential assistant's tenure. Looked at most broadly, it might appear that the presidential assistant role is purely a staff function, and it is quite often defined as such at many institutions. In this version of the role, the presidential assistant does not stand in authority over any administrative unit, perhaps other than the president's office staff, and has neither the budget nor personnel responsibilities normally associated with line positions in organizations. Put bluntly, presidential assistants are not to be confused with assistant presidents or vice presidents. They are, very often, the seniormost staff people on campus, but are staff nonetheless.

In contrast to this analysis, however, 51.8 percent of the presidential assistants in the NAPAHE study view themselves as senior administrators on their campuses. How does this come about, and what are its implications for higher educational administration in general?

CHARACTERISTICS OF PRESIDENTIAL ASSISTANTS WHO ARE SENIOR ADMINISTRATORS

The distribution of presidential assistants who self-describe as senior administrators is anything but random. To investigate what might correlate with this status, two response sets were analyzed and compared with the sample at large. In the first, I looked at respondents who said that their job was conceived as senior management at their institutions. The second examination was of those who indicated holding specific line responsibilities.

Those who say that they are seen as senior administrators were significantly more likely to:[2]

- Be at higher Carnegie-level institutions (Master's, Doctorate, Research)
- Be at institutions offering doctoral and master's degrees as their top offerings
- Hold bachelor's degrees in humanities, social sciences, and education
- Have more years in their jobs than the other presidential assistants
- Have higher base salaries than is usual for a presidential assistant
- Have more interaction with board chairs and board members
- Be male

In contrast, those presidential assistants who reported having formal line responsibilities (see below) share only the years in position and salary variables as significant. They are not clustered in institutional types, they have no particular backgrounds, they do not interact especially with trustees, nor are they predominantly male or female.

It is possible to speculate on the implications of these findings, but only to speculate. The correlation with years on the job is consistent with the notion described below, namely, that one way to attain senior status is to associate with senior administrators for long enough. The association with institutions of greater complexity may reflect the presence of more opportunities to assume responsibilities for major functions, or the relatively greater organizational "weight" of the president's/chancellor's office at larger institutions. The preponderance of humanities, social science, and education backgrounds may be evidence for what has been argued all along as the virtues of a liberal education: no job on campus may require greater flexibility, ability to learn quickly, or multistranded approaches to solutions. The issue of gender is one that pervades much of the data in the NAPAHE study. Curiously, the number of men and the number of women in the sample who describe themselves as senior administrators are nearly equal: 202 women and 203 men, compared to the sample, which is more than two-thirds female. The work, salary, and level of responsibility of the men and women in this category are not distributed evenly, as the chapter on gender makes clear. At the same time, we must remember that these are self-reported data, and question whether men in this often ambiguous role called "assistant to" might want to overstate their organizational power.

ROUTES TO SENIOR ADMINISTRATIVE STATUS

Presidential assistants achieve senior administrative status in four principal ways, which I will call "routes" to that status. In the most straightforward instance—and this is true for 42.7 percent of those who self-describe as senior administrators—the presidential assistant also has line responsibility and another title to go with it. A second route to senior-level responsibility can come about as a result of reorganization within the administrative structure that leaves a presidential assistant in a new position vis-à-vis the other senior administrators. While this may only be a temporary circumstance, the experience of authority obtained during that time may leave vestiges when the assistant returns to the staff role. An alternate route to a senior level occurs when a president formally pronounces the presidential assistant to be invested with authority: "He/she speaks for me," as promulgated in an introduction, memo, or some other fashion. In the fourth route, the presidential assistant achieves senior administrative status informally, by processes of association, personal behavior, or other combinations of circumstances.

LINE RESPONSIBILITY

A presidential assistant may be appointed to that position while already in charge of an administrative unit, or may be appointed to such a management position as a result of being a presidential assistant. So, for instance, a director of public relations can be appointed as presidential assistant (sometimes "special assistant") and retain supervisory function while assuming additional tasks for the president.

A PA may also receive a line title and function as a result of new skills acquired or new needs arising at an institution. The president may come to realize that someone should be given responsibility for the management of a function that is either new (e.g., response to new legislative mandates) or of enhanced importance ("We have this need. Would you like [*sic*] to do it?"). Among the more common "new" skills in recent years is expertise in electronic technology. Accordingly, a presidential assistant might become vice president for information services, or a similar title, while maintaining functions within the president's office. Sudden departures of key administrators, particularly at smaller institutions without great personnel depth in most units, may offer the chance for a presidential assistant to move into a role, either as a stopgap measure, or in a more permanent way. As an example, a presidential assistant might fill in as an interim director of human resources and might retain supervisory functions over that or kindred units after a permanent director is put in place.

Holding a line position while being a PA may create awkward situations when administrative units are in contention for valued items, be they financial resources, space, or the ear of the president. It may be difficult for the presidential assistant to avoid the appearance of favoritism on behalf of his or her own unit and to advocate for that unit at the same time.

This process of assuming a line position provisionally is a prime example of the overall administrative flexibility that the position of presidential assistant provides. It is possible that there is a historic process in which presidential assistants' roles are created to fill newly emerging administrative functions; we may see this process in action in such temporary assignments.

ASCENT BY MEANS OF REORGANIZATION

Administrative reorganization can provide openings in the organizational structure that the presidential assistant can fill, provisionally or permanently. For instance, a president may need to spend exceptional amounts of time off campus in fund-raising pursuits and may shuffle responsibilities among the senior staff so as to see that all functions are covered. All functions, that is, except coordinating the senior staff. This task may fall to the presidential assistant, who consequently acts as a peer toward the vice presidents/vice chancellors.

Reorganization may also create the need for new supervisors of functions, and the presidential assistant may be in an ideal position to take on those responsibilities. This then becomes an instance of the first route, holding line responsibility. For instance, as seen in chapter 13, "Juggling Jell-O: Other Duties as Assigned," the emergency assumption of responsibilities to meet some campus crisis can result in the presidential assistant retaining permanent supervisory responsibility over crisis management teams.

FORMAL ANNOUNCEMENT

There is always some murkiness in the presidential assistant role: is this person an avatar of the president, a high-level gopher, or both? One way to cut through this confusion is to have the president declare formally that the presidential assistant is an authoritative representative of the president and that, correspondingly, the presidential assistant's word carries presidential weight. This announcement may be made at the time that the presidential assistant is appointed or may come later. Obviously, it must be public for it to have impact. Sometimes, a title change may be used to signal this relationship, for instance, associate to the president.

Such an announcement has a double edge to it. The president, in so announcing, becomes able to be in two places at once. The presidential assistant, by contrast, must fully submerge his or her own opinions in order to represent the president faithfully. To an extent, all presidential assistants face this latter predicament. Those who are formally anointed as the voice of the president, however, may find it difficult ever to speak "off the record."

INFORMAL ASCENSION TO POWER

Probably the most common road to senior status is an informal one. Recall that 57.3 percent of those who self-describe as senior administrators do not hold a second, line position. Rather, by being in the circles of power for a long enough time, by having access to all the highest-level information of the institution, or even control of that information, and by associating as a peer with the clear bearers of authority, the presidential assistant may obtain de facto senior administrative stature. This stature may never be crystallized into a formal role and may or may not be widely perceived by the institution as a whole. It may also depend a great deal upon the personality of the presidential assistant in interaction with those of the president and, especially, the vice presidents.

The leadership style of the president is critical in this equation. One of the most common functions performed by presidential assistants is to serve as staff for the president's cabinet. This, of course, entails being at the table as the cabinet discusses the policy issues of the institution. It is in this arena that a presidential assistant can begin to accrete elements of authority, if certain circumstances exist. First is the extent to which the cabinet functions as a truly deliberative, decision-making body, either by consensus or by voting, as opposed to a forum in which vice presidents learn what the president has decided. If decision making is very tightly controlled by the president, the presidential assistant's cabinet role may be no more or less influential than that of anyone else at the table, save the president.

Next is the question of whether the presidential assistant has a voice in the deliberations that take place, either when opinions are asked or even when votes are taken. This may be established formally at the outset, or may occur informally, or may even change as time goes on. In my own experience, cabinet conversations moved toward consensus and the cabinet was rarely polled for its opinions. For example, two or three years into my tenure, one such poll took place and when the rounds had been made of all the vice presidents and I was obviously next in line, I first hesitated until the president requested that I offer a vote. From that time on, I was in the roll call, though these were rare.

At times the presidential assistant's input may be requested if the presidential assistant has special expertise or information regarding the subject in question. There may need to be a decision made about the follow-up to a project that the presidential assistant has managed. For instance, our cabinet regularly discussed how to apportion staff salary increases with regard to internal equity and market forces. I conducted the statistical analyses of the staff salary structure that informed this debate. As a result, I had a better comprehensive understanding of that structure than anyone at the table, and my views had consequent weight. Or, the presidential assistant may develop a specialization such that his or her opinion is the most informed at the table. Perhaps the presidential assistant is assigned to legislative relations. The presidential assistant may consequently lead a discussion concerning institutional responses to lawmakers. A PA who is also the board secretary may speak with authority when trustees are the subject of discussion, perhaps, for example, about plans for trustee officer succession.

None of the circumstances above are necessarily ones in which a presidential assistant assumes formal authority. One can imagine a situation in which the presidential assistant is thanked for his or her information and tacitly told to go back to taking the minutes. If, on the other hand, the president is highly consultative and nonauthoritarian and if, moreover, the vice presidents accept the rules of the conversation and do not feel threatened by the presidential assistant, it is possible to engage as a peer in policy deliberations.

The senior stature of a presidential assistant may be enhanced by taking on the role of mentoring new vice presidents. If the presidential assistant has had long experience in the administration, it may make good sense to ask the presidential assistant to offer advice to a new vice president about how to accomplish tasks, whom to go to and whom not to go to, and to fill in the vice president about the essential folklore of the institution. It may be wise for presidential assistants to volunteer for such duty, both as a means of assuring critically needed good relationships, as well as creating an appearance, at least, of equality.

Senior administrative authority may also be a covert matter. One of the advantages of having a presidential assistant with executive capacities is the way it allows the president to be away from campus, typically on fundraising missions. Life goes on while the president is away, and decisions may need to be made. Even in this age when technologies allow everyone to be contacted anytime, it may be more effective for the presidential assistant to make the decision, particularly if its gravity is relatively slight. The presidential assistant must feel confident in his or her knowledge of the president's position on the matter at hand. The president, likewise, must be willing to delegate such authority. One can imagine that such a procedure has a built-in braking function: making the "wrong" decision (contrary to what the president would have done), or stepping far beyond the boundaries and making a large decision, is not likely to happen more than once.

Another covert form of senior authority is probably quite common. Presidential assistants are often involved in policy discussions with their presidents, either at the president's instigation or that of the presidential assistant. In these conversations, a policy position enunciated by the presidential assistant may be taken up by the president. In subsequent, broader discussions of this issue at hand, the presidential assistant's role in the creation of the policy may be hidden. Learning to accept a situation like this with grace is a critical skill for a presidential assistant. Nevertheless, when such a scenario is played out, the presidential assistant has performed a senior administrative function, albeit without formal authority to do so.

Finally, there are cases in which a presidential assistant is assumed to be a senior administrator, acts like a senior administrator, and is always seen in the company of senior administrators. The resulting perception by all in question is that the presidential assistant is indeed a senior administrator. The presidential assistant must be aware that this is going on. In addition, the president and vice presidents must have no objection to such a perception being held. We should expect this situation to be most common where a presidential assistant has been a long time in the role, and the data bear this out.

PRESIDENTIAL ASSISTANTS, INFLUENCE, AND POWER

The survey data also allow us to see whether the presidential assistants who describe themselves as senior managers differ in any significant ways with regard to their effect on the central management of their institutions. All the responses are self-assertions of authority or influence; one might expect those who say they are senior to also say they are important. Nevertheless, those particular variables that are significant give us a portrait of what senior management function may be like, even without senior-level authority. In contrast to the rest of the sample, the presidential assistants who self-designate as senior management are significantly more likely to feel that:

- Their suggestions are typically acted upon
- They derive influence from a wealth of contacts outside the institution
- Other senior staff pay attention to what they say
- Faculty pay attention to what they say
- The president pays attention to what they say
- They derive power and influence from their ability to broker ideas
- Their writing is important
- Their grasp of policies and procedures gives them power

Presidential assistants who hold formal line authority share all these responses except those of faculty attention, presidential attention, and influence derived from grasp of policies and procedures. Perhaps this indicates that those with line positions, being more functionally specialized, have a more circumscribed range of influence. Insofar as those line titles are almost never in the academic realm, it may be unsurprising that little faculty influence is claimed. The fact that presidents do not pay them as much attention may suggest that they are not as often in the consultative, confidant roles that presidential assistants often play.

Overall, these findings are consistent with the pathways outlined above, most especially the "accretion" and "appointment" models. In each case, we would expect presidential assistants to be exerting power by influence, by special knowledge or contacts, and through being in the position to move ideas around an organization. When the presidential assistant is "authorized" by formal presidential action, we would certainly expect faculty and senior staff to "pay attention to what I say," since "what I say" is to be taken as presidential utterance.

PEEKING OUT OF THE SHADOW

An initial working title for this volume was "In the Shadow of the President." How is it that we have presidential assistants living in the shadow of the president, over half of whom assert that they are seen as senior management? Being seen with the president at all may be reason enough. Over a third of the entire sample (35.3 percent) also have line positions, undoubtedly in full view. Of the rest, who lack titles with formal authority, many have roles of influence that are played at the highest institutional levels. It may be the case that the relative transparency of institutional decision making enables some presidential assistants to be seen as senior managers, as they are always or frequently known to be engaged in policymaking discussions. When that role is officially communicated to the campus at large, or when by dint of long service the presidential assistant is assumed to know all that is important to know, we have situations to which the shadow metaphor is less well suited. What presidential assistants do may not be well known, but this need not make them obscure.

NOTES

1. With assistance from John Cummins, former assistant chancellor, University of California, Berkeley; Carol Lysne, former executive assistant to the president, St. Olaf College; Mary Jo White, executive assistant to the chancellor, University of Colorado, Boulder.

2. Significance here represents chi square differences at the .100 level.

⫿

A CAREER AS
A PRESIDENTIAL ASSISTANT

Elizabeth Wright Schoenfeld[1]

I remember the day in 1980 when I told a faculty mentor that I wanted to be a university president's assistant. He didn't quite see the point. But to me, the job was intriguing. Although the qualifications were unclear, the role appeared to require broad education, political and structural understanding of the academic enterprise, and skills in problem solving, writing, and communication. Could it be interesting enough to sustain a career? Would there be any room for advancement? Was a career even conceivable in a nation where university presidents serve an average term of about six years?

It doesn't take much experience on the job to speak with authority concerning the first of those questions. The position has great potential to be interesting over the course of a career because of its variability and the complexity of responsibilities, often consisting largely of "other duties as assigned." Indeed, these positions are as changeable as the personalities of the president, the assistant, and the institution in which they labor.

At an American Council on Education–sponsored session for presidential assistants (PAs) in 1988, the chair, James Scally of the University of Kansas, described the challenges of the position, which can be demanding and unrelenting. He indicated that he had been in the role for twelve years and was on his third chancellor. There were groans from the assembled crowd; it sounded like a lifetime. Despite the fact that few PAs dispute the stimulating nature of the job, few long-serving PAs actually planned to stay so long and they seem reluctant to admit that they are in a career position. As Scally said, "Is a job like this a career in itself or is it a way station? Does it lead anywhere, or is it actually a dead end? Most likely, it is what we choose to make of it." Shall we make it a career?

WHAT IS A CAREER PA?

The term "career" implies an opportunity for consecutive progressive professional achievement or a profession for which one can train, which may be undertaken as a permanent calling.[2] This chapter explores how each of these elements is increasingly common to the experience (if not the plan) of presidential assistants in higher education.

The comprehensive national survey commissioned by NAPAHE in 1995 indicated that half of the 800 respondents were the first to hold their position, and nearly a third had held the job less than two years. Twenty-one percent had been in the role for more than a decade. Ten years later, a less rigorous snapshot survey of 107 presidential assistants attending a NAPAHE conference in 2005 revealed that just 25 percent had held the job less than two years, a significant difference, and a quarter had been in a PA position for ten years or more, several for more than twenty years. While some served consistently with the same president, well over half of those had worked with multiple presidents and interim presidents. The 2005 survey did not capture whether individuals had served at multiple institutions, though that too is an experience shared by PAs around the country.

DO TITLES DEFINE A CAREER PATH?

The titles used for presidential assistants aren't particularly descriptive and provide little indication of a career ladder. People across the nation with different titles seem to be doing the same things—and people with the same title are doing different things. Change and maturity in the role may not be reflected in a change of title. Because the available titles are vague, advancement in a PA role may not be apparent to the university community.

The College and University Personnel Association, which maintains a comprehensive listing of titles and salaries for higher education, does not clearly define presidential assistant titles. Thus the range of salaries for "presidential assistant" in the annual salary survey is wide and difficult to interpret. NAPAHE makes no attempt to create definitive job descriptions because the institutional uses vary so broadly. The NAPAHE website (www.napahe.org) includes a sampling of job descriptions from around the country.

The association has also examined the question of title progression, and considered creating a standard for the profession. One attempt is included in table 11.1 below. However, the practice among institutions is not consistent and is not congruent with these definitions. In some institutions, for example, the executive assistant title may reflect an updated title for the executive secretary; at others, it is a senior staff member as described below. A career might progress through the titles, or might begin at any level and stay there.

CAREER EVOLUTION

A typical PA career, like many careers, tends to evolve organically, without reference to a plan. Personal and professional circumstances, opportunity, and luck are common threads in the stories of five PA careers discussed in this chapter. While none of the five trained for their career paths as such,

Table 11.1. Presidential Assistant Titles and Responsibilities

Proposed Title Progression	Typical Range of Responsibilities (May Build on Previous)
Administrative Assistant to	Executive secretary responsibilities, including clerical support, scheduling, travel, office management, etc.
Assistant to	Primary professional support for the president, which may include producing agendas, policy research, writing, managing office staff, etc.
Special Assistant to	May be differentiated from "Assistant to" by specialized portfolio, such as diversity, legislative, public information, special events, speechwriting.
Executive Assistant to	Senior policy-level assistant or advisor; may have additional management responsibilities, including staff supervision, management of agendas and governance processes, representing the president at public functions, membership in the president's cabinet.
Executive Associate or Associate to	Prefix and title denote a higher level of administrative or policymaking/advising responsibility.
Chief of Staff	Advisor to the president, manager and gatekeeper of the office of the president, coordinator of the divisions reporting to the president.

all have taken advantage of professional development opportunities provided by NAPAHE, the Association of Governing Boards' Workshop for Board Professional Staff, other institutes and professional associations for their specialized responsibilities, and the growing research about higher education administration. Each story demonstrates strategies for designing a career that involves consecutive progressive achievement without leaving the position alongside the president. A permanent calling? Time will tell.

CAREER IN A SINGLE INSTITUTION: SURVIVING TRANSITION

The most natural career for a presidential assistant would be at a single institution. An assistant's knowledge of the university and its programs, people, and politics, and familiarity with the community potentially provide long-serving and new presidents with a broadly useful institutional memory. Within an institution, the position often is filled for a limited term by faculty or administrators interested in pursuing or furthering an administrative career, or aspiring to a presidency.[3] It also initially may be a special project position that evolves, or a promotional opportunity for experienced clerical staff.

Most positions in higher education require specific professional credentials. Former University of Michigan PA Constance Ewing Cook acknowledged that "people who serve as presidential assistants, however, have a wide range of professional backgrounds; their roles typically are tailored to their own skills and to the working style of their presidents and their institutions' current needs" (Cook, 1993). For a PA, higher education, the coin of our realm, is no substitute for experience.

Veteran PA Art Wallhausen humbly posits that one of Gilbert and Sullivan's greatest characters—Sir Joseph Porter, K.C.B., in *HMS Pinafore*— would make a good patron saint for presidential assistants:

> You may recall that Sir Joseph became First Lord of the Admiralty with no discernable qualifications, very much like the real-life politician who was satirized by Gilbert and Sullivan in their wonderful song, "When I Was a Lad." Of course, presidential assistants are not rulers of the Queen's Navy, but like Sir Joseph, PAs have usually risen from the ranks without any special training, and like Sir Joseph, they often have significant opportunities for participating in the leadership of our institutions. (Wallhausen, 2001)

Yet there is no training for being a presidential assistant more reliable than on-the-job training. Art noted that in his early years, he felt "as unprepared as Sir Joseph, who had never seen any ship but his junior partner*ship* in a law firm."

Wallhausen came to Southeast Missouri State University in 1984 as a news bureau director with no prior background in higher education. Like Sir Joseph, he served an apprenticeship of sorts, "polishing up the handle on the big front door." Like Sir Joseph, he acquired a grip on essential knowledge, did a professional job as director of the news bureau, and, like Sir Joseph, he *says* he never thought of thinking for himself at all.

But during his two years in the news bureau, Art received some interesting projects from the president's office. After success with one short-term project dealing with community relations, he was invited early in 1987 to serve as the president's first assistant, a role that he had never contemplated. As the president's assistant, Art was useful in continuing to handle the news bureau, and became secretary to the cabinet and the president's administrative council. This president also gradually invited him to attend and participate in meetings of the board of regents, including their closed sessions. Art served his first president for two and a half years before the president left the institution; thereafter he was "inherited" by two interim and three "permanent" presidents.

Because presidential terms average six years nationwide, planning a career as a presidential assistant means planning for transition. Successful transition of an assistant to a position with a new president is unpredictable. The incumbent assistant, particularly a well-paid assistant, is often the first to be pushed out in the revolving door of the presidency.

Before Father Tim Healy left the presidency of the University of Notre Dame, he provided sage advice to his successor: that a new president should resist the urge to pare back support staff in an attempt to look administratively lean to "signal efficiency to the campus community" (Malloy, 2003). Healy recognized that appropriate staffing is indispensable for an effective presidency. His successor, Edward Malloy, understood, gradually building the president's staff from one to three.

President Malloy acknowledged important factors in defining whether a PA can anticipate a long career at a single institution. "I have learned that the relationship between a president and his or her assistants must be open, confidential, and frank and be based upon mutual respect and trust. Every president needs a reliable sounding board, a second set of eyes or ears, a person to pass on news about unpleasant realities, and an encourager in times of difficulty. When and if this fundamental dynamic breaks down, it is not in the president's interest to continue the relationship" (Malloy, 2003).

From a new president's perspective, there is considerable benefit to working with an established assistant. However, a president with an option to continue with the predecessor's assistant has issues to consider, not the least of which is that, depending on the exit of the predecessor, continuation of the former president's PA may be tenuous politically. Given the importance of the role, a new president who finds an experienced assistant in place should think twice before dismissing the former president's assistant out of hand. A president should assess areas in which the president's office needs support and how many individuals are needed to provide that support. Then he or she should determine, perhaps after a trial period, whether the current staff are in a position to help or if the political landscape mandates looking to new staff within or outside the institution for primary assistance.

From the incumbent PA's perspective, survival relates to important factors that are not within his or her control. Wallhausen, eventually titled as associate to the president, notes that first and foremost, one must have good luck in the situation that led to the previous president's departure and in the board's choice of a new president. His advice:

- The PA can't control such factors as a president whose basic method of operation is to get rid of all traces of the previous administration. This is especially true if the former president is leaving under a cloud and the new president believes a housecleaning is essential to his or her own success.
- The PA can't control his or her fate if the new president has a special focus that is not within the current PA's expertise or has a longtime assistant he or she wants to bring to the new institution.
- The PA may be pressed into change if the new president comes from within the institution and the current PA's history with that new president won't sustain continuation in the role.
- The PA and the president might have incompatible personality inventories—the assistant's will always be the one to yield. (Wallhausen, 2001)

Although the impact of a president's decision to change assistants is experienced personally, the decision is not necessarily an adverse judgment about a PA's abilities as much as a statement of the president's perceived needs. Transition also is a decision point for the assistant to consider. Is the position still interesting and challenging? Will the change in leadership bring desirable new responsibilities? Do I want to continue in this role given the personality and priorities of the new president? What career steps are open to me? Am I in a position to move from the institution or location?

Having served with six presidents at his university, Art Wallhausen's service is instructive to those who might like to survive even one presidential transition within an institution to sustain a longer career. He suggests the following eight strategies:

1. Secure the high ground on the campus by playing a key role in an important process, such as developing agendas for the executive staff.
2. If possible, become invaluable, or at least visible to governing board members, who may then put in a good word for you with the new president.
3. Demonstrate to the new president the depth of your knowledge and dedication and loyalty to the institution and the presidency.
4. Be involved and helpful to the candidates during the search process. They will recall your kindness.
5. Accept any job with good humor, even if it's only carrying the president's purse or luggage. The tips are small, but the benefits are great.
6. Remember the role and needs of the spouse, who may appreciate the importance of the relationship for both.
7. Get there as early as possible. Demonstrate your knowledge of the institution and the issues as early as possible. During the search is an ideal time.
8. Seek and/or accept line responsibility and make certain that your job description reflects all responsibilities added along the way. It may provide you a golden parachute if a new president wants a new assistant. (Wallhausen, 2001)

A presidential assistant facing transition must be realistic, flexible, thick skinned, and ready for a career change. Or, if a career as a PA is contemplated, one must be ready for a move to another institution.

ASSISTING ONE PRESIDENT: A MOVING EXPERIENCE

Learning how to use an assistant to best advantage can take time. A new president ideally wants someone who can be trusted from the start, someone who can support strengths and overcome challenge areas. Thus, while the practice isn't the norm, many presidents, particularly those who are moving from one presidency to another, have taken staff with them when they move, maximizing the chances of a successful relationship.

Chancellor Nancy L. Zimpher hired her first presidential assistant, Kathryn St. Clair, at the University of Wisconsin–Milwaukee from the UWM School of Education in 1998. Like Zimpher, St. Clair had served as a coordinator of field experience and student teaching in a college of education, and Zimpher considered their common skill set while searching to fill the vacant PA position. She decided to trust her instincts and took a chance on Kathryn rather than hire any of the candidates with experience in a president's office. Kathryn, after fifteen years in the UWM School of Education, moved to the Office of the Chancellor, created a new set of office procedures, and acquired the softer skills involved in serving a chief executive officer.

Five years later, Dr. Zimpher accepted the president's job at the University of Cincinnati and faced another decision point: continue to staff the new office with the very senior administrative team that had served her predecessor president so well for two decades or recruit new talent. Dr. Zimpher decided to invite Kathryn to move with her to Cincinnati and to build a new team using many of the elements that had evolved through much trial and error in Milwaukee. Kathryn's husband had just retired from his long career, their son was married and on his own, and there were no big obstacles to an out-of-state move at the time. She welcomed the opportunity for continued service to a "president on the move" and to apply what she had learned in the first PA position to a new, more complex higher education setting.

While an imported assistant is unable to offer knowledge of the local university community, an established relationship holds distinct advantages. At Cincinnati, Kathryn was able to play a key role in the presidential transition because she knew President Zimpher so well—her style, beliefs, values, preferences. Kathryn served as "translator" for the vice presidents and other members of the president's cabinet, and the president trusted her assistant to represent her well. If asked, St. Clair would not claim that she is a career assistant, but rather a higher education professional with a great opportunity to serve a dynamic and charismatic leader in two different settings.

Another story of career development is told by the experience of Jennifer Raeke, who has worked alongside President John D. Stobo for nineteen years. Their partnership began in 1988, when he was chair of the Department of Medicine of the Johns Hopkins University School of Medicine and physician in chief of the Johns Hopkins Hospital. With five years of administrative secretarial experience at Hopkins and an associate's degree, Raeke's initial role was as his administrative support person, managing the office staff, juggling his calendar, and handling his extensive travel schedule. Six years later, when Dr. Stobo became chair and chief executive officer of the then-new organization of Johns Hopkins HealthCare, LLC, he asked her to come along as a member of his new team. This move came with a promotion and the sometimes difficult jump out of the secretarial designation to management. Raeke's advancement to executive assistant to the president (a position later renamed chief of staff) came in November 1997, when Stobo accepted the presidency of the University of Texas Medical Branch in Galveston, Texas.

Like Kathryn St. Clair, Jennifer Raeke attributes her success in the chief of staff role to the fact that she and Dr. Stobo share many of the same values. She has a clear understanding of his views and opinions on most issues. "I don't always agree with him, but I'm always pretty sure what his thoughts, decisions, and reactions will be" (J. Roeke, personal communication). This knowledge is imperative given the fact that she is expected to help advance the president's agenda. In her position, Raeke has taken the lead on various initiatives that influence and help shape the culture of the institution. She has chaired several university-wide committees, and recently was named public information officer for the university, responsible for handling all open records requests.

When Dr. Stobo announced his plan to step down from the presidency of UTMB in August 2007, Raeke began looking forward to the next phase of her career. She has completed a bachelor's degree, and expects that the experience and skill she has gained over the last nineteen years will serve her well in her next career move.

If longevity is any measure, six presidents at Southeast Missouri State University have been well served by a predecessor's assistant. Wallhausen was able to bridge the gap between presidents, whether by dint of personality, experience, or a combination thereof. Yet, the experiences of St. Clair and Raeke indicate that a personal comfort level of trust and capability between president and assistant can outweigh the home-team advantage. With presidential transition as a constant, an experienced PA can provide stability in the Office of the President. But presidential assistants recognize that there are no guarantees of continuation after a transition, particularly because the relationship with the president is so central to success.

SURVIVAL IN A "MOVING" INSTITUTION

In 2009, Mary Ann Shallberg had been at the University of Houston, Clear Lake (UHCL), for twenty-nine years through four presidents. Her narrative illustrates the changeability of a career in a multilayered institution and the applicability of Wallhausen's survival strategies.

Shallberg, executive associate to the president at UHCL, is clearly a career presidential assistant. She has served in a PA role since the early 1970s, when University of Houston (UH) president Philip G. Hoffman invited her to move from the development vice president's office to the president's office in an interim capacity. A few months later, she accepted a permanent position on the president's staff.

Shallberg's first role in higher education after earning a bachelor's degree in business education was, like Jennifer Raeke's, as an executive secretary. The transition to PA came during the ten years she served with President Hoffman. UH was in a period of rapid growth and change, evolving from a single university to a system of four universities by 1974. When Hoffman became president of the University of Houston System in 1976, Mary Ann served as his special assistant until he retired in 1979, and upon his departure, as assistant to the interim president and staff to the search committee.

Early in 1979, Mary Ann and her husband moved from near downtown Houston twenty-five miles south to Nassau Bay, Texas, just four miles from UHCL, which had opened its doors in 1974.[4] UHCL's founding chancellor, Alfred R. Neumann, had previously been dean of the College of Arts and Sciences at UH, so they knew each other well. When his assistant announced her retirement later in 1979, Neumann approached Mary Ann about her interest in the position. He particularly noted the excitement of being part of a new university—and the potential benefit of a much shorter commute. Although the decision was difficult, she decided to make the move to UHCL in 1980, and never looked back.

In her twenty-nine years at UHCL, Shallberg has had the unique opportunity to work with each of the institution's four presidents, whose terms ranged from two to nine years.[5] The second and fourth presidents came as the result of national searches, which she staffed, and the third as a two-year interim appointment that extended to four years. In each case Mary Ann was able to play a key role in the transition. While each president came with his own leadership and management style, she has made a career of approaching the transitions with a positive attitude and a sense of excitement and opportunity.

Although being a career PA was not part of a plan, as it evolved, Shallberg sensed that this was meant to be her life's work. Participation in the evolution of the new, upper-level university and watching it grow from the ground up, working directly with the president to help make things happen, created a changeable career that has been meaningful, never boring, always challenging.

SURVIVAL AND EXTERNAL RECRUITMENT

It is not uncommon for a president to look externally for an assistant. As noted above, there may be no one available on staff with the specific experience desired, there may be a political need for a fresh start, or a president may have an established, trusting relationship with a colleague who can be imported. The opportunity to draft a position description tailored to the president's needs creates a framework for success. Presidents have differing needs for assistance based on their own strengths and agendas. With over two thousand presidential assistants at universities and colleges across the country, and others with needed skills in and outside of higher education, there are many experienced professionals to draw from.

Shallberg's experience, shifting positions within a university system where professional relationships are facilitated, mirrors the first thirteen years of my PA career. My first assignment was with the University of Wisconsin System. I had been working on Vice President Katharine Lyall's staff in the Office of Academic Affairs on a variety of policy issues, and she designated me as her assistant when she was promoted to executive vice president. After five years, I was loaned to the University of Wisconsin–Rock County, to serve as interim dean. Shortly after I returned, Lyall was promoted to interim president and then president of the UW System. Following in the footsteps of her predecessor, she did not hire an assistant, but relied on the new executive vice president for the primary coordination and support for her presidency. Thus, my first transition occurred as I began to work with her successor, Executive Vice President Ron Bornstein.

Bornstein brought to his position experience and a continuing interest in public broadcasting, a field in which I had no experience. After about a year, when he was ready to focus some attention on that interest, Bornstein was key in creating a new assistant position for Chancellor Lee Grugel of the University of Wisconsin Colleges, to which I moved. This left Bornstein free to hire someone with the experience he needed. For me, the position provided new responsibilities, including work as a legislative liaison, and did not require a move to a new location. Incidentally, I had served as a representative of the UW System administration on the search committee that had recommended Grugel for the chancellorship.

After working as the chancellor's special assistant for five years, I occasionally considered the next, inevitable transition of leadership, and determined that this would be my last assistantship. Life as an assistant—much less an assistant for life—is not for everyone. Though the responsibilities of the position can be immense, one rarely receives public credit for accomplishments, making it difficult to shape a resume around them. The PA must be a quintessential team player internally, but may appear to the public to be just a caddy. As one matures in the role, being in the background may get a little old.

Constance Ewing Cook said it well: "We need an odd combination of a strong ego and no ego at all. Ours is not the best job for people who need a great deal of thanks or recognition. Most of our work goes on behind the scenes—unobtrusively, if we are doing it well. When President Clinton's Chief of Staff, Thomas (Mac) McLarty, III, asked for advice from people who had previously held his job, they suggested that chiefs of staff fare best if they have 'a passion for anonymity.' Similarly, James Scally, former assistant to the chancellor of the University of Kansas, once joked that the emblem of our presidential-assistants' organization should be a shadow on a field of gray" (Cook, 1993).

Despite the fact that skills in this complex job are doubtlessly increasing, the uncertainty about a next career step seems to increase the longer one serves in the position. For those who try to plan a next step in case they don't survive or don't want to survive a transition, NAPAHE conference sessions about "life after being a PA" inevitably draw questions from individuals who are uncertain what they are now qualified to do. If a PA has a broad portfolio, specific subject-matter expertise begins to fade, making it difficult to be competitive for a position limited to any one of those specialties. As assignments become more diverse over time, one becomes more of a generalist; experience is broad, rather than deep.

SURVIVAL OF THE UNEXPECTED

While some have been successful in planning a career around a PA position, oftentimes a career just happens. To prove John Lennon's maxim that "life is what happens to you while you're busy making other plans," my last impetus to move came with the unexpected death of my chancellor, Lee Grugel, one Wednesday night. The idea of taking on a completely new set of responsibilities, with my young children (then seven and nine) and ailing parents, was daunting. After working with the interim and new chancellor and on special projects for the UW System during a transition year, I was drawn to an executive assistant position at a single institution across the country. Western Washington University president Karen Morse had just lost her assistant of four years to a promotional opportunity at another university and there was no heir apparent on staff.

Having worked for a total of six executives, I took care to check references for Dr. Morse, calling her former assistant and a president who had worked with her, and I interviewed the campus as it interviewed me. The challenge of a university with several new responsibilities in an otherwise familiar role appeared to be an ideal transition to the "different" position I had imagined for my future. Experience at a comprehensive university was new to me. The new position added speechwriting, membership in the president's cabinet, and line responsibilities suitable to the role and to my experience. The president seemed committed to acquiring a colleague rather than a gofer.

Nine years later, the role continues to evolve. As I inevitably move toward another transition, it is with an appreciation for the variability of the role and the professional strength that comes from adapting to the needs of an institution and its president(s).

CONCLUSION

Presidential assistantship can be a temporary career step or a career in itself. A career in this work entails breadth of knowledge, flexibility, willingness to be in a support role and to take on a variety of new responsibilities as they present themselves.

While the PA position will likely remain primarily a temporary career step, as George Washington University president Stephen Trachtenberg has stated, the rise of career PAs says a lot about the modern presidency (Trachtenberg, 2000). Demands on the presidency are increasing. The need for expertise in the presidential assistant role to cope with those demands is also increasing.

In addition to the characteristics common to successful assistants described elsewhere in this book, there are some common threads that enable one to sustain a career. The most critical of these is the vitality of the trust and relationship between the president and the assistant. Those PAs who survive presidential transitions are successful because they have an opportunity to prove that they are loyal to the institution and the presidency and can be useful to the next president. Those who transition with their presidents have been party to building a strong relationship. Those who move to a new institution, with or without the president, find a president who appreciates that the skill set of an assistant is not necessarily contextual.

Definition of a career as a presidential assistant is chiefly about the ability to transition through change. In our colleges and universities, at least, change is a constant, so there are many opportunities to hold the potential of a career up for examination.

NOTES

1. With assistance from Art Wallhausen, retired assistant to the president, Southeast Missouri State University; Kathryn St. Clair, former chief of staff, University of Cincinnati; Jennifer Raeke, executive assistant to the president, University of Texas Medical Branch, Galveston; Mary Ann Shallberg, executive associate to the president, University of Houston, Clear Lake.

2. Merriam Webster online dictionary, www.m-w.com/dictionary/career.

3. For a list of presidents who have been PAs, see http://chronicle.com/jobs/2000/04/2000040703c.htm.

4. Located adjacent to NASA's Johnson Space Center, midway between Houston and Galveston, Texas, UHCL is an upper-division and graduate institution with an enrollment of more than 7,700.

5. The chancellor and president titles reversed in the mid-1980s. Neumann from 1980 to 1982; Dr. Thomas Stauffer from 1982 to 1991; Dr. Glenn Goerke from 1991 to 1996; and Dr. William Staples from 1996 to present.

REFERENCES

Cook, C. E. (1993, July 7). Gatekeeper, facilitator, gofer, flunky. *Chronicle of Higher Education*.

Malloy, E. A. (2003, November/December). Those indispensable presidential assistants. *Trusteeship*. Association of Governing Boards, p. 5.

Trachtenberg, S. (2000, March 18). Keynote remarks at the NAPAHE Annual Meeting.

Wallhausen, A. (2001, February). Surviving the revolving doors of the presidency. Speech given at the NAPAHE Annual Conference Presentation.

⑫

WHAT DO PRESIDENTIAL
ASSISTANTS DO NEXT?

Anthony R. Ross

A loyal and able assistant can be the president's most important staff member. He or she belongs to the president, for the assistant's role is defined exclusively in terms of the president's best interests. Without the president, the assistant has no professional existence. A good assistant performs everything, from the menial to the magnificent: running errands, opening doors, driving to off-campus meetings, representing the president, and, at times, acting as vice president without portfolio. Assuming the assistant has no significant line responsibility, freed of specific administrative duties, he or she will have a gestalt view of the institution and be able to respond more in keeping with the president's interests (Fisher & Koch, 1996).

Earlier chapters have dealt with the many and varied tasks of the presidential assistant (PA), how PAs live in the shadow of their presidents (or not), the career paths of PAs, and gender issues affecting PAs, as well as the qualities of PAs. In this chapter I focus on preparing for life after the presidential assistantship.

In the opinion of Fisher and Koch (1996), the presidential assistant truly has no identity of his or her own. The PA's existence is defined "exclusively in terms of your [the president's] best interests." No matter what the presidential assistant did prior to assuming this important and sensitive role, once agreeing to become a PA, his or her identity merges with the president's. Almost instantly, the PA is transformed into a senior and valuable staff person who becomes the ears and eyes of the president. At once, the PA is messenger and bearer of tidings, gifts, and even bad news as well as the voice behind the throne. Presidential assistants are also thrust into such roles as chief negotiator, mediator, town crier, ambassador of goodwill, and institutional leader. With such a complex list of qualities and skills as a backdrop, many presidential assistants, when thinking of leaving the position, ask, "What do I do next?"

THE PRESIDENTIAL ASSISTANT
AND PROFESSIONAL DEVELOPMENT

As is noted above, assuming a position as a presidential assistant can be like giving up one's own life. The president's thoughts become the PA's thoughts, the PA's actions are those of the president, the manner of dress, style, and even speech patterns begin to resemble those of the president. One's entire identity becomes so closely associated with that of the president that at times PAs can finish sentences for their presidents (and often do).

Given an existence that is so closely connected to the president, it is easy to see how one can lose or at least submerge one's own identity and not attend to one's own professional development. And yet, it is imperative for the PA to pay attention to self and the continued professional growth that is essential to the role. To do so ensures that the PA is serving the president and institution well by staying informed and up to date in those areas that relate to student issues, management, leadership, higher education policy, and the political environment. Increasing one's knowledge base while enhancing skills for the role of PA can be simultaneous preparation for opportunities beyond that of presidential assistant.

Such professional development can take several forms. One is to identify those professional associations and organizations that best suit one's interests and needs, to attend their national conferences, and to commit to become an active member. Active membership is the lifeblood of any professional association and is an excellent way to cultivate the network that can be vital to taking the next career steps. The most obvious place to start is membership in the National Association of Presidential Assistants in Higher Education (NAPAHE), an affiliate of the American Council on Education (ACE). However, broader professional interests could and should also be pursued. Other associations might provide a sense of connectedness to specific functional areas or disciplines. As examples, one might also become active in Student Affairs Administrators in Higher Education (NASPA), the National Association of College and University Business Officers (NACUBO), the Council for Advancement and Support of Education (CASE), the Society for College and University Planning (SCUP), the Association for Institutional Research (AIR), or a discipline-specific association. Attending the annual meetings and conferences, taking time to network, and attending sessions outside one's specific interest area are ways to enhance one's skill set (exploring such topics as public speaking, enhancing writing skills, mediation, etc.). It is even more valuable to become known by making presentations or becoming an officer in the organization. Above all, it is key to continue to listen and learn.

In many instances, presidential assistants do not avail themselves of professional development opportunities because they "censor" their participation by thinking that their presidents will not support them, or that there are no funds available to underwrite participation, or that they cannot be away from the campus for any length of time for fear that "the place will fall apart without me there." This may well be poor thinking. First of all, most presidents understand the value of professional development and networking and may well have the budget to support travel requests, provided wishes are made known. Second, it is a mistake for a PA to think that he or she is indispensable. The campus (no matter the issues) has been around for a long time and was successful before the PA's arrival, and no doubt that success will continue long after the PA leaves.

A second major mode for professional development is participation in one of the national institutes for those in leadership roles in higher education. Among the best known are the Harvard School of Graduate Education Management Development and Institute for Educational Management programs, the HERS program at Bryn Mawr College, and the ACE Fellowship program, as well as comparable programs put on by the various professional associations (e.g., NASPA's James E. Scott National Academy for Leadership and Executive Effectiveness).

Some of these programs are more extensive or selective than others. This is less important than the fact of deciding to participate in a growth and professional development opportunity. Professional development, like charity, begins at home.

THE DECISION TO MOVE ON

All presidents have decisions to make about their length of tenure at an institution. So, too, does every PA. If a decision to move on is truly that of the president, then the PA is fortunate. If the president is in a "good place" in terms of the opportunities that await him or her, the PA in a "good place" as well, either because of general institutional success or because the PA may be able to accompany a mobile president.

If the president has just received the dreaded "vote of no confidence" from the faculty, or the board has asked for the president's resignation, then the circumstances surrounding the PA's decisions become more difficult. It is only reasonable to suppose that a PA would fail along with a failing president. On the other hand, we know of many PAs who have remained in their posts through several, even many presidents. Nevertheless, a wise PA maximizes his or her potentials through ongoing professional development.

Whatever the circumstances of your president's departure from your institution, knowing that a departure decision is forthcoming from the president or the board should trigger a similar decision-making process for the PA. One should already have begun the process of considering all the options: from trying to stay in the current role with the hope that the new president will agree, to making plans to move to another position on campus, to deciding to leave the institution altogether. Depending on one's relationship with the president and the circumstances surrounding the departure, the president may be able to offer the PA guidance for that next position.

It is vitally important to be sure that one leaves the PA position under good circumstances and that all relationships are intact. Even if the parting is less than amicable, there should be an agreement with the president to provide a supportive recommendation when it comes time for reference checks from a future potential employer. An agreement for a supportive reference is essential and is no less than what the president will have negotiated for himself or herself with the board of trustees or regents. Regardless of the submerged identity noted early, PAs, especially long-term ones, also can have considerable power and influence. It may be important to use that position and influence to gain what the PA needs in a case of sudden career crisis. Whatever the decision, a PA must remember that there is choice in the matter. It is imperative to plan accordingly.

UPDATING THE RESUME AND USING NETWORKS

Rule number one: always keep a resume or vita updated. It is wise to do so, especially in light of frequent speaking engagements both on and off campus. Rule number two: read and become familiar with the *Chronicle of Higher Education*. It is the only comprehensive weekly source of news affecting colleges and universities worldwide, and it also contains what is probably the single most referenced classified section in all of higher education. When updating a resume it is wise to let another colleague, family member, or friend review it, to catch typos, read for content, and offer pertinent changes. There is only one chance to make a good first impression, and the cover letter and resume are it in most cases. One's resume will be a symbol of the quality of one's work.

A good cover letter is essential. It is important to remember that, absent a face-to-face meeting, the cover letter (letter of application, letter of interest) is the only chance to convey the skills and qualities that make the writer an outstanding candidate for a desired position. This is one of the rare times in life where it is appropriate to focus on accomplishments—indeed, to boast. This posture is also far removed from the basic background positions of a PA, and it may be difficult to assume. However, a letter that highlights accomplishments, qualities, and skills, while demonstrating how those attributes match the reader's needs, is essential.

Once it has been determined that it is indeed time for a change, one should inform certain members of one's professional network of friends and colleagues as to the decision to move on. Keeping certain colleagues informed about plans ensures a cadre of supporters who might be able to assist along the way. Even when considering opportunities outside higher education, colleagues on one's own campus as well as on other campuses can provide vital contact information and insight into opportunities that one might otherwise miss out on. Remember, the nature of the work and contacts of presidential assistants extends far beyond that of the campus, with many of those contacts reaching into corporate boardrooms. These networks should be used to assist in getting that next position.

UNDERSTANDING THE SPECIAL VALUES OF BEING A PA

A presidential assistant has the distinct advantage of seeing the university as a whole. This perspective may be in contrast to that of vice presidential colleagues whose view of the university is constrained by the various departments and units that comprise their divisional responsibilities. The various assignments given to presidential assistants call for institutional vision, which further allows the PA to be the ultimate generalist for the campus. This vision of the sense of the whole sets the PA apart from others on the campus and makes the PA and his or her skill set valuable to the campus.

A broad and well-defined skill set as well as the ability to see the big picture and to inspire others to hold a shared vision (usually that of your president) are just a few of the leadership traits presidential assistants possess. The trick becomes one of recognizing these traits in oneself as well as one's ability to communicate them to a future employer. It is important to conceptualize and acknowledge that these are skills that are valuable in other settings. Whether on campus in a different position, at a new institution in a new role, or in the private sector, these skills are needed and in demand. The critical issue in making the change is understanding the values brought to the institution by the work of the PA, and to see how such values apply to the new opportunity.

MAKING THE MOVE

A presidential assistant, given the usual access to information as well as a level of understanding about the nature of life as a staff member or administrator, should encounter no career surprises. Like most other staff members or administrators on a campus, PAs are "at will" employees, meaning that they serve "at the pleasure of the president." Generally speaking, PAs have no tenure, unless they are tenured faculty members with "retreat rights" to the faculty. The more one understands the nature of the conditions surrounding one's employment, the fewer surprises will be encountered, and the better prepared one should be to move ahead with career goals.

Regardless of the length of service at the institution, a PA should always be in the process of preparing for the next job, at least mentally. A look at coaches and managers of professional sports teams can help to clarify this concept. Coaches and managers understand that their jobs are temporary (many are fired midseason) and they will tell you that they are "hired to be fired." While they make every attempt to win every game, they aren't always successful and eventually are either fired or asked to resign.

Even a PA who has been at the current institution for an entire career should always place himself or herself in the position of having options. The president does! Much as a PA must be prepared for whatever circumstances may arise regarding the president's office or the institution, so must a PA be prepared for the unexpected regarding his or her own future.

WHAT'S NEXT? WHERE TO GO? WHAT TO DO?

Thanks to career exploration, professional development, understanding their own value, preparation, and networking, presidential assistants do leave the ranks of those who "live in the shadows of their presidents" and begin to cast their own shadows. The following are examples, from my personal experience, of the kinds of transitions that have been made:

- From presidential assistant to director of a major national or regional commission
- From presidential assistant to faculty member
- From presidential assistant to associate provost or dean
- From presidential assistant to official with the U.S. Department of Education
- From presidential assistant to vice president in a corporation and back to university vice president
- From presidential assistant to president of a university

Among the sixteen contributors to this volume were PAs whom we now find in the roles of:

- Vice President for Advancement
- Vice President for University Relations
- Vice President for Student Affairs
- Director of Institutional Research
- President

This is but a partial list of those presidential assistants who have made successful transitions to significant positions both on and off campus. In most of the instances listed above, the transitions were planned as part of conscious career decisions. And in the cases where the transitions were not planned, the former presidential assistants were prepared for and open to such opportunities, once they became evident. Not all were actively searching, but some were; not all possessed doctorates, but some did; not all knew what opportunities awaited them, but all were prepared. The skills learned in their roles as PAs prepared them for the next steps in their respective careers.

Those currently in the role of presidential assistant, as well as those aspiring to be, or those who are just curious about the PA position, should know that PAs possess "the right stuff" to succeed at many things. Just what is "the right stuff?" It is a combination of attributes and traits that authors such as Bennis and Nanus (1985), Bolman and Deal (1995), Kotter (1996), and others have identified as necessary to succeed in positions of leadership: developing a vision for what can be, exhibiting effective communication skills, and having the ability to listen, to inspire others to action, to see and understand the big picture, to plan and work various aspects of the plan, to know when to let others lead, and to seize the moment.

These are all skills that presidential assistants possess, and these are skills that are widely valued in the workplace. Whether on or off campus, what matters is that a PA understands his or her value and knows that he or she adds value to the institution, the community, or the company. Once all of this is understood, a PA never need worry about "What do presidential assistants do next?"

REFERENCES

Bennis, W., & Nanus, B. (1985). *Leaders: The strategies for taking charge.* New York: Harper & Row.

Bolman, L. G., & Deal, T. E. (1995). *Leading with soul.* San Francisco: Jossey-Bass.

Fisher, J. L., & Koch, J. V. (1996). *Presidential leadership: Making a difference.* Phoenix, AZ: American Council on Education and Oryx Press.

Kotter, J. P. (1996). *Leading change.* Boston: Harvard Business School Press.

13

JUGGLING JELL-O:
OTHER DUTIES AS ASSIGNED

John Cummins[1]

"Your job is like juggling Jell-O." That was one of the comments I received from the executive vice chancellor shortly after becoming the assistant chancellor–executive assistant at the University of California, Berkeley, twenty-four years ago. Three chancellors later, and hopefully somewhat wiser, I believe there is no better description of this position.

In a job that is almost wholly dependent on one's relationship with the chief executive, the duties evolve chiefly on the basis of what the boss needs at any given time. The job may be defined more specifically to include office management, speechwriting, policy analysis, board management, and public affairs (to name a few), but an essential component of doing the job successfully is effectively handling other duties as assigned. These assignments are largely unknown as one assumes the position. They can fall anywhere on the "significance" continuum, and they are conferred on the basis of the trust and confidence the chief executive has in the assistant.

What is it that the boss really wants? It is a given that he or she wants a high level of competence in the more defined parts of the job. Putting that aside, in an optimal relationship the boss wants someone to talk to; someone who does not have a personal agenda, an axe to grind; someone who will speak the truth when it needs to be spoken; and someone who is totally loyal. It is in that context that the "other duties as assigned" emerge.

What are some of these jobs? I will organize the following examples into the categories of Serious Crises, Less Serious Crises, Designated-Hitter Situations, and the Mundane.

SERIOUS CRISES

These are the most obvious, the most intense, and the most time consuming for either short or extended periods of time. About one year after moving into my position, large-scale protests erupted over apartheid in South Africa and the demand that the university divest itself of any financial holdings with corporations that conducted business in that country. In what appeared to me to be an offhand comment by the chancellor to the campus police chief, he stated that I was to be involved in all meetings dealing with campus protest. That "conferral" of authority quickly turned into situations where I was required to make on-the-spot decisions about police strategy and tactics, for which I had no preparation. That trial by fire led to my having permanent responsibility for the coordination of responses to all campus protest.

As a result of my extensive involvement with the campus police, I and the vice chancellor for business and administrative services were the first ones called when any campus emergency occurred. In my tenure, this included earthquakes, a fraternity fire with fatalities, power outages, a student homicide, street riots, one of the largest urban fires in the United States (working with the parents of a student who died in that fire, and with faculty and staff who lost their homes), a bomb threat that required evacuation of the entire campus, a hostage situation involving a large number of students in a local bar, an attempt on the life of a chancellor and his wife in their campus residence that led to the killing of the intruder, and numerous protests, large and small. Depending on the given event, all my normal work ceases for periods of days or weeks.

LESS SERIOUS CRISES

Matters in this category do not involve health and safety, but they can be equally as time consuming as those that do. Research fraud, embezzlement, conflicts of interest, and scandals in intercollegiate athletics are examples. While there are internal procedures and policies for dealing with these matters, the presidential assistant is often pulled in to monitor the progress of an investigation, keep it on track, review confidential documents, and be a liaison with the public affairs office. Since it is assumed by the relevant parties that the assistant speaks for the chancellor or president, matters such as these can be very time consuming. Often, the amount of information one needs to know is gargantuan, and the president or chancellor may not have time to absorb it fully. It is often the assistant's job to condense large amounts of information into a concise summary to assist the chancellor in making a decision. One case of alleged inappropriate governmental activity involving research funds took a full five years to resolve and spanned the terms of two chancellors at Berkeley.

DESIGNATED-HITTER SITUATIONS

This category is beyond the typical representational role that the assistant is expected to fill. It is more than the attendance at a meeting or ceremony that the president cannot attend. It includes authority, however undefined and ambiguous, and a responsibility to address the situation and make it better. It involves issues that fall between the cracks in an organization.

The matter already discussed about protest management is an example. Another example was the management of the Naked Guy at Berkeley. This involved a student who had a long-standing belief that clothing was unnecessary at all times. He began attending classes one fall stark naked. Since we neither had a local ordinance on nudity nor a section dealing with this in our student conduct code, we did nothing to address this, hoping that the student would come to his senses on his own accord. When that did not work, and when the practice seemed to be spreading, I quickly convened a meeting with our police chief and legal counsel. We drafted an executive order banning nudity on campus and then used the student conduct process to remove the Naked Guy from campus for failing to obey that order.

Here are some other examples:

- The chancellor decided to make organizational effectiveness a priority for the campus. This grew out of his own frustration with the bureaucracy and the many complaints that he had heard on this subject. After several months of learning and analysis by a high-level committee, it was decided that a Center for Organizational Effectiveness should report to me. This decision was made because it signaled the importance of the effort by having the center so close to the chancellor. Also, the center could not be located in line units that were in fact part of the problem.

- A state law on protection for whistleblowers, and a broadening of current university policy on misuse of university resources to include all inappropriate governmental activity, led to the creation of a Local Designated Official on each University of California campus, who has overall coordinating responsibility for the investigation and resolution of these matters. The law and the policy are so broad that no one individual (auditor, controller, etc.) quite fits the bill, so again, this responsibility was given to the presidential assistant.

The first example is something that would fit the typical job description for an assistant. It shows initiative in dealing with something that is highly unusual and unpleasant and where something clearly must be done. The other two examples are reminiscent of the television commercial for a cereal where the older brother says to his friends, "Let Mikey try it." They also pose a potential land mine for the assistant because these responsibilities are highly visible, could easily lead to failure, and are very time consuming. One must be careful in taking on such responsibilities because they can seriously undermine the ability of the assistant to be available to meet the specific needs of the chancellor or president. Thus, it is very important that the assistant and the president jointly understand and are clear about the repercussions of the assistant taking on long-term assignments.

THE MUNDANE

This is the catchall category. I include in this things that need to be done whether they are requested or not. They run the gamut from the trivial to the very important. I have dusted, fluffed pillows, taken home and washed hand towels, picked up trash in front of the administration building. I have rewritten the speechwriter's speeches; consulted off-line and on with reporters when they got the story wrong; lobbied legislators; consoled donors whose children were not admitted; and chaired and served on search committees and other committees and task forces dealing with admissions, strategic planning, athletics, financial controls, and a host of other matters. Many of these are common assignments for assistants and reflect the level of trust and confidence that the chancellor has in his or her assistant.

DOING THE JOB

With such a mishmash of duties and responsibilities, how does one possibly prepare to deal with them? In my case, there was no training. No one had actually played such a role, and mine evolved on the basis of luck and circumstance. I would assume that this is the case for others in similar roles. The NAPAHE survey indicated that 52.5 percent of assistants surveyed indicated that they were the first to hold the position at their institutions.

Certain psychological characteristics or personality traits are helpful. Again, they are not essential. There are many ways to do these jobs. I can only speak for myself. A story from my own life might best illustrate my traits or characteristics:

As a teenager, I spent many hours playing baseball. The field where we played was so large that it was possible to fly model airplanes at the same time that two baseball games were going on. While I had never flown these planes, I observed people who did many times. One day, a father and his young child were attempting to fly such a plane. The father would start the small gasoline engine, have his son hold the tail of the plane on the ground, and then run back, pick up the guy wires and attempt to get the plane airborne. Each time he did this, the plane simply nosed over on the ground and the engine died.

Out of frustration, the father approached us and asked if anyone knew how to fly these planes. I immediately volunteered. The father started the engine. I picked up the guy wires and told him to release the plane. Instantly, the plane was airborne. As I turned in a circle, with the plane whirring around and around, I thought to myself, "Why not try a few tricks?" This turned out to require much more skill than simply getting the plane up in the air. I flicked my wrist quickly, hoping that the plane would dip and then soar skyward. The plane certainly did dip, but it never regained its upward motion and it crashed into the ground. My reaction to an even more frustrated father: "There must have been a defect in the plane."

What does this anecdote say about me, and how does it relate to doing my job? First, there cannot be any fear about stepping forward to deal with problems even though one has limited knowledge. There is a fine line between taking risks and being foolhardy, however. Attempting tricks with no knowledge at all was foolhardy. Sidestepping responsibility by blaming the plane was simply wrong. I always keep this story in mind when dealing with the myriad issues I confront at any given time. Act. Do not take an unacceptably high level of risk. Take responsibility for the outcome. The second of the three dicta is the most difficult because a final judgment on this can only be made after the fact. This is the essence of why the job of presidential assistant is more art than science.

THE ART OF JUGGLING JELL-O

Assume that taking action, evaluating the risk of a particular strategy, and taking responsibility are the basic tenets of administrative juggling. Also assume that one likes juggling—that uncertainty, ambiguity, a low level of frustration tolerance, and avoidance of anxiety are not at the top of one's list of psychological descriptors. Then what? How does one do the job? Obviously, one has to prioritize. In doing so, there are two critical factors, in my opinion: time and gut instinct. Certain matters will inevitably be driven by deadlines. If a deadline cannot be met, get help or tell the boss it is impossible. Other matters must be addressed immediately because of their consequences. The emergencies are obvious. Others one learns over time by doing the job and knowing the culture and history of the institution. Relationships with key faculty and donors, an unhappy mayor, a reporter who has the story wrong, a simmering conflict between two senior managers, a rumor that there may be a significant NCAA violation—these matters cannot wait until other, more routine assignments are completed. Sometimes these may not be one's own hot-button issues, but they may well be for the boss.

There are also ways of carrying out responsibilities day in and day out that assist mightily when it is necessary to juggle several things at once. These are the lessons I learned and relearn as I continue to do my job. These are the commandments, the self-imposed disciplinary steps, the focused practices over time that increase the chances for success when one is given that one additional chunk of Jell-O to keep in the air along with the other five that are already there.

1. First, get the facts. As obvious as this statement is, it is surprisingly easy to forget in the heat of the moment. A piece of information from an informed source can seem self-evident and lead to a chain of events that is embarrassing for the individual and the institution because the facts were not checked. This is the *sine qua non* of being an effective assistant.
2. Think, don't react. Another way to put this is: solve the right problem. Because the assistant is expected to solve problems and because there can be a tendency to wrap up issues quickly and move on to the next

ones, one must think carefully to make sure the right problem is being addressed. Do not solve one problem and create another in its wake. I learned this lesson for the first time when I was four years old. As I sat on the curb waiting for the kindergartners and first graders to come home from school, one little girl finally came down the street. It had been raining during the day, and she complained to me that her mother made her wear boots. I told her that I could solve that problem if she took off her boots. She did, and I threw them down the sewer. Needless to say, I faced a much bigger problem an hour later when her mother phoned mine.

3. Be clear on where authority resides to handle the issue. It is not uncommon for senior administrators to want the assistant to solve their problems. Sometimes there is no choice about this because the chancellor/president may tell the assistant to do so. If there is a choice, one can work with the senior administrator to help solve the problem but should avoid taking that problem on as one's own.

4. Consult with others. In most cases, there is an opportunity to try out a strategy for handling a problem before actually implementing it. Assistants need their own trusted advisors. Who they are will vary depending on the problems confronted. Use them. One will never be sorry, and humility will rise on one's list of prized virtues.

5. Envision the desired outcome and work backward. This is a nifty tool because it enables one to get a handle on those groups and individuals who will not like that outcome. They have to be dealt with as part of the solution, not after one thinks the problem is solved.

6. Focus on getting the job done, not on getting the credit. If possible, it can be helpful in the long run to make sure that someone else gets the credit. This can smooth relationships when the next issue comes along.

7. Move things along. Do not worry about developing the perfect solution. Do not be another bottleneck. By the time problems get to the assistant's desk, it is certain that they have been vetted at other levels in the organization to no avail.

8. Related to number seven above, get back to people and let them know where things stand. More than anything else, people who ask for help want to be listened to. They need to know that someone is listening and cares about their problem. Updating them frequently on how one is dealing with the issue lessens their frustration.

9. Put it all in perspective when completely overwhelmed. I used several psychological devices: I reminded myself that it is possible to deal

with only one thing at any given moment. I picked an issue and I dealt with it. I reminded myself that the campus had survived other more serious crises, and it would survive many more long after I was gone. I envisioned myself being calm no matter what happened. I focused on listening and not being the first to offer a response.

10. Show up; observe for yourself. I quickly learned the importance of this in the context of campus protests. Firsthand knowledge based on observation is very different than the knowledge one gains from after-the-fact reports.

11. Put in the time. It should be obvious that one cannot do this job on a nine-to-five basis. It is important to understand that time is not under the assistant's control. One should expect to work weekends and evenings and even be called back from vacations from time to time, depending on the urgency of the situation. Extreme demands on one's time may not occur often. When they do, there should be no resentment. It comes with the territory.

12. Take good notes and learn how to write quickly, clearly, and concisely. This is very helpful in clarifying thinking as well as being able to communicate quickly and clearly to a variety of audiences, internal and external.

13. Have a sense of humor. Almost any opportunity for self-deprecation or levity should be taken advantage of, particularly in difficult situations. It can lighten the mood, calm tempers, provide perspective, and move the agenda along.

In concluding, let me now return to the executive vice chancellor who coined the juggling terminology and remind the reader that assistants to presidents and chancellors are not the only jugglers in an organization. Most senior managers, and particularly chancellors and vice chancellors, have as much or more coming at them as any assistant. The difference of course is that they have more staff than the assistant does to get the jobs done. Nevertheless, what singles out the best of these jugglers is the state of mind one brings to the task.

The executive vice chancellor enjoyed juggling. He genuinely liked the challenges that confronted him and looked upon each situation as a game of chess. He analyzed what was before him, was very strategic in his approach, had great confidence in his abilities, and was decisive. But most important, he loved the challenge. He did not find his job wearying but rather thrived on it. If an assistant is going to be a good juggler, he or she had better like juggling and enjoy practicing that skill.

NOTE

1. With assistance from Lane Estes, vice president for administration, former assistant to the president, Birmingham Southern University; Brien Lewis, vice president for development and alumni, former executive assistant to the president/secretary to the Board of Trustees, Winthrop University; Robert Berdahl, president, Association of American Universities, former chancellor, University of California, Berkeley; Patrick Hyashi, former associate president, University of California System; Michael R. Smith, former assistant chancellor for legal affairs, University of California, Berkeley; Peggy Kelly, psychologist, University of California, San Francisco, Medical Center.

AFTERWORD

Mark P. Curchack

Senior executive, speechwriter, complaint handler, office manager, personal manager, board secretary, fund-raiser, and other things we have not discussed—affirmative action officer, government affairs coordinator, director of planning, director of public relations, and more—does any one presidential assistant (PA) do all of these things? Probably not, at least not all at once. But many, indeed most, play many of these roles over the course of a year or the course of a career. Some PAs are specialists and are so titled: special assistant for public relations, human resources, special projects, and so on. The greater number, however, are generalists, the Jell-O-juggling administrators whose jobs are so difficult to define. As participants in the NAPAHE annual meetings have long observed, we all do different things and we all have much in common. Perhaps this is why the authors in this volume cannot agree on which Gilbert and Sullivan operetta best captures the position.

Perhaps this is also why the role has become so widespread so quickly. We take as a given that college and university presidents lead ever-busier lives with more time away from campus. Thus, having a nimble administrator capable of filling a wide variety of functions becomes more important. The fact that a goodly number of PAs have served on the same campus under several presidents, often facilitating the search for their boss's successor and handling the transition, argues on behalf of the position's centrality in the management of the modern American college and university. Still, it is a transitional position for some, who often move upward in the realms they left to serve in the president's office—student affairs, public affairs, planning, institutional research, institutional advancement, and so forth. A few, not otherwise intimidated by what they see their bosses doing, go on to be presidents, generally by way of a deanship or provostship on the way.

For many PAs who have discussed these things over the years, our job is the best on campus, giving us access, and sometimes influence, over all that happens, with no two days, or even two hours, quite the same. Some thus choose to stay in the role, for the actual adventure that it can bring. PAs have the chance to make a difference in their institutions, whether or not this is ever acknowledged. The satisfactions may need to be internal, but they can be immensely satisfying.

In the two appendixes that follow, we hear the views of this role from two former PAs, as given in addresses to the NAPAHE annual conference. Pamela Transue, the president of Tacoma Community College, one of those former PAs not dissuaded by the experience, looks at the parallel between the PA role and that of the Renaissance courtier, and gives us some of the history of NAPAHE in the process. Second is one of the most beloved of those whom we in NAPAHE have known, James Scally, who left the PA role to become a dean shortly before his untimely death. His fictionalized "day in the life" essay, most PAs will agree, is not so far-fetched.

APPENDIX A

IN THE GRAND TRADITION OF THE COURTIER: THE PRESIDENTIAL ASSISTANT[1]

Pamela Transue

It is remarkable to think that such a lively and interesting organization as this one could emerge from the simple gesture of picking up the telephone and calling a few strangers. I had been in my position as special assistant to the president at the University of Washington for four years when I decided that something needed to be done to combat the isolation I felt. Those of us in the presidential assistant role had no professional association, no professional development opportunities tailored to our responsibilities, no conferences focused on our roles, and no clear career paths. That's why I was calling strangers. I knew that hundreds if not thousands of other presidential assistants must be out there, but I had never met one. Instead, we were toiling in perhaps not-so-splendid isolation. That revelation was enough to cause me to pull the Higher Education Directory from the shelf.

I was very fortunate in the people I contacted that day. I decided to start with institutions similar in mission to the University of Washington because I thought I would have the best hope of finding kindred spirits there. I picked a few universities with appropriate geographical representation and began calling. Remember, there was no e-mail, no fax machines, no voice mail. I know that is hard to imagine, but it's true. (I had one of the first PCs on my desk. It had less memory than a typical wristwatch today, and I spent five days in Boca Raton at IBM's expense learning how to use it.) In any case, I called the switchboard at various universities and asked to speak to the assistant or special assistant to the president. I ended up speaking with twenty-four startled people. They seemed uniformly delighted at the thought that there might be others like them out there who would enjoy a professional association of some kind.

From that group, four people seemed particularly enthusiastic about moving forward: Carol Berthold from the University of Illinois, Tim Gilmour from the University of Maryland, Carol Herrmann from Penn State, and Jim Scally from the University of Kansas. The five of us formed a steering committee and held an initial meeting at the O'Hare Airport Hilton in Chicago. We decided that our best chance for success lay in affiliating with a large association and holding our meetings in conjunction with their annual convention. The American Council on Education (ACE) seemed an obvious choice since we would probably all be attending anyway and since it would allow us to connect with other types of colleges and universities, large and small, public and private. With the steering committee's concurrence, I contacted Marlene Ross at ACE. She expressed interest and we began planning for our first national meeting, which took place at the ACE convention in Washington, D.C., in January 1988.

Our steering group expanded to include John Fallon of Saginaw Valley State University and Sheila Clemon-Karp of Clark University, and soon thereafter Jane Buie of Loyola and Mary Ann Shallberg of the University of Houston at Clear Lake. These were excellent additions to our team, and with the momentum thereby created, NAPAHE began to really take off. I am very proud to have been involved with such a remarkable group of peers and to see the great success that has followed those initial efforts.

As you know, being the alter ego to a president is a challenging, fascinating, and yes, occasionally stressful position. In order to be effective, you have to know how your president would think or react, and what he or she would say or write about any and every situation. You have to disagree without offending when you think the president is about to take a misstep, and you need to be so thoroughly trustworthy that the president has a safe place to vent or at least to be freed from the constant pressure to be unrelentingly diplomatic. You must show your best face in every situation because whatever you do reflects on your boss. You must be able to anticipate likely outcomes of interactions and to ensure that access is both open and controlled, a clear contradiction that you must nevertheless manage gracefully. Your job can be all-consuming. I knew it was time for me to think about moving on when I bought about $100 worth of groceries at a local supermarket and signed the check "William P. Gerberding" [then the University of Washington president—ed.].

As many of you know, my next position was a campus presidency with the title of executive dean at Portland Community College. I had developed a passion for the community-based mission of community colleges that has lasted to this day. My ability to succeed in my position in Portland and for the last nine and one-half years as president of Tacoma Community College owes a great deal to the excellent apprenticeship opportunity I had for seven years at the University of Washington.

I don't know if any of you remember, but there was an article on presidential assistants in the *Chronicle of Higher Education* a few years ago (Montell, 2000). The article opened with a story about Helene Interlandi, the assistant to Steve Trachtenberg, the president of George Washington University. She had to find a home for a life-sized bronze hippopotamus that her president had acquired. It has since become a major campus presence and good-luck charm. The article talked about the many and varied responsibilities of presidential assistants in higher education. Your former association president, Mark Curchack, was asked why he would leave a faculty position for his role, and said: "Faculty, in many respects, are extremely narrowly focused. As executive assistant to the president, I get my bloody little hands into almost everything."

A few years ago, I happened upon an article in a Phi Theta Kappa publication that I found revelatory. In this article, John Clemens explores the art of "followership," using the great sixteenth-century work by Baldassare Castiglione called *The Book of the Courtier* as his text. In this book, Castiglione re-creates a series of conversations occurring in the court of the Duke of Urbino in 1507. During the course of several evenings, various courtiers engage in a series of conversations with the Duchess on the qualities of character and behavior that constitute the ideal courtier. As I read the article, I experienced a little frisson of recognition. The parallels between the qualities of the good courtier and the qualities of the good presidential assistant were unmistakable. But why should we have to reach back five hundred years to find advice on how to be successful in our roles? As I thought about this, I realized that there are thousands of publications and presentations on leadership, but none that I could come up with on followership—except, of course, for *The Book of the Courtier*.

When it was published, *The Book of the Courtier* was immensely popular, as was its author, Castiglione. As John Clemens says, the book served as a "kind of policies and procedures manual for courtiers-in-training. And it was history's first unabashed 'how to' book, providing lessons in everything from dealing with a tyrant boss to how to give advice, be a good listener, give feedback safely, follow orders, enforce rules, harness the sins of pride and arrogance (in both yourself and your leader), and how to keep the peace" (Clemens, 1996–1997, p. 39).

Castiglione begins his book with a letter to his friend, Alfonso Ariosto, who has encouraged him to compose this work on the art of the courtier. In this letter, he says the following:

"Now, you have asked me to write my opinion as to what form of Courtiership most befits a gentleman living at the courts of princes, by which he can have both the knowledge and the ability to serve them in every reasonable thing, thereby winning favor from them and praise from others: in short, what manner of man he must be who deserves the name of perfect Courtier, without defect of any kind" (Castiglione, 1959, p. 11).

Castiglione goes on to describe the history of the Court of the Duke of Urbino and why it forms the perfect venue for a discussion of the virtues of good courtiership. In this educated and refined environment, the courtiers were accustomed to joining the Duchess after dinner in a kind of salon, where discussions on a variety of topics were interspersed with music, dancing, and ingenious games. It was in this context that the topic of the perfect courtier was chosen.

One of the first characteristics discussed was the importance of making a good first impression: "Consider, then, how important that first impression is, and how anyone who aspires to have the rank and name of good courtier must strive from the beginning to make a good impression" (Castiglione, 1959, p. 32). I think everyone in this room knows how important that is. Anyone meeting you in any circumstance who knows what you do for a living will see you as a reflection of your boss. If you are grouchy, or unkempt, or surly, or unhelpful, or curt, or addle-headed, that will reflect on your boss. I remember needing to contact another member of my Rotary Club when I was serving as program committee chair. The person in question was a moderately successful attorney with an open and friendly manner. When I tried to contact him, however, I met up with the imperious assistant. "Who is this calling?" "Pamela Transue." "What did you want to talk with him about?" "A program for Rotary." "Mr. X is very busy. Give me the details and I'll speak with him about it." To which I replied, "I need to get back to the speaker this afternoon, so I really need to talk with Mr. X. It will only take a minute." Imperious assistant: "I handle these matters for Mr. X." Me: "So I can't talk with him?" Assistant: "No." My opinion of the attorney in question plummeted, and I haven't liked or trusted him since. What kind of a person would want to give that kind of impression to potential clients or to anyone else, for that matter?

But what of the character of the good courtier? As Castiglione advises, no Caspar Milquetoast should apply: "Therefore, let the man we are seeking be exceedingly fierce, harsh, and always among the first, wherever the enemy is; and in every other place, humane, modest, reserved, avoiding ostentation above all things as well as that impudent praise of himself by which a man always arouses hatred and disgust in all who hear him" (pp. 33–34). And later he advises, "But let the Courtier be eloquent when it suits his purpose and, when he speaks on political matters, let him be prudent and wise; and let him have the good judgment to adapt himself to the customs of the countries where he happens to be; then, let him be entertaining in lesser matters and well spoken on every subject. But, above all, let him hold to what is good; be neither envious nor evil-tongued; nor let him ever bring himself to seek grace or favor by resorting to foul means or evil practices" (Castiglione, 1959).

I hope you will agree that such a list of character traits, though daunting, eloquently articulates the virtues of an excellent presidential assistant. One must be both fiercely loyal and self-effacing, eloquent yet prudent, adaptable, knowledgeable, circumspect, discreet, and at all times ethical. Because the courtier serves as a mirror of the prince, he must be well-spoken. For, in Castiglione's words:

> What is most important and necessary to the Courtier in order to speak and write well is knowledge: because one who is ignorant and has nothing in his mind worth listening to can neither speak nor write well. Next, what one has to say or write must be given a good order. It must then be well expressed in words, which words (if I am not mistaken) must be proper, select, lustrous, and well formed, but above all be words which are still used by the people. (p. 54)

Finding that balance between "lustrous" and using language that is easily understood can be challenging, as all of you know. Among my duties as Bill Gerberding's special assistant were drafting correspondence, writing speeches, and formulating written policies. Bill was one of the brightest and most articulate people I have ever met, so meeting his standards was not easy, even with a Ph.D. in English. I remember two gaffes with clarity even to this day, because Bill was clearly embarrassed by something I had failed to catch. In the first instance, I had used the word "precipitously" when I should have used "precipitately." The meaning I hoped to convey was that a decision had been made in too much haste. The proper word was precipitately, since precipitously should be used only to denote physical steepness or a metaphor of physical steepness, as in "a precipitous drop in interest rates." The second faux pas that I recall with mortification was referring to people from Scotland as Scotch instead of Scots.

It will come as no surprise that Castiglione stresses the importance of prudence and discretion:

> Our Courtier must be cautious in his every action and see to it that prudence attends whatever he says or does. . . . Therefore, in all that he does or says, I would have our Courtier follow certain general rules which, in my opinion, briefly comprise all I have to say. And the first and most important of these is that he should avoid affectation above all else, as the Count rightly advised last evening. Next, let him consider well what he does or says, the place where he does it, in whose presence, its timeliness, the reason for doing it, his own age, his profession, the end at which he aims, and the means by which he can reach it; thus, keeping these points in mind, let him act accordingly in whatever he may choose to do or say. (pp. 97–98)

As a presidential assistant, one has a wealth of knowledge about the political and strategic underpinnings of decisions. And though the tendency to gossip is anathema for someone in this role, the material for doing so is ever present. Other people know this, and they will do their best to extract it from you—charming you with their wit, cajoling you with flattery, plying you with liquor. People want information about what is going on at the top of the organization, and you are a major repository. You must resist the urge to share what you know. Doing so will ultimately erode the trust that is so essential to your role.

As for using your position to seek favors, Castiglione says:

> Rarely or almost never will he ask of his lord anything for himself, lest his lord, not wishing to deny it to him directly, should perchance grant it to him with ill grace, which is much worse. And when asking something for others, he will be discreet in choosing the occasion, and will ask things that are proper and reasonable; and he will so frame his request, omitting those parts that he knows can cause displeasure, and will skillfully make easy the difficult points, so that his lord will always grant it, or do this in such wise that, should he deny it, he will not think the person whom he has thus not wished to favor goes off offended. (pp. 111–12)

Because of the nature of the relationship that exists between presidential assistants and their bosses, it is usually very difficult for a president to say no to a favor, even if he or she thinks it is unwise or inappropriate. Requests for favors can easily create a level of tension or unease between presidents and their subordinates, so they should be carefully considered. Before requesting a leave or support for a significant professional development opportunity or a salary increase, be sure you have gathered sufficient information on how this will benefit your institution and/or allow you to better perform your duties as presidential assistant. Consider the pros and cons from the point of view of your boss, and then present your case. Allow room for "no," and if you receive that answer, get over it and move on. If you feel undervalued, it is probably time to start looking elsewhere.

If you are seeking a favor for someone else, keep in mind that your boss is aware that you are taking advantage of your relationship. That is probably acceptable on occasion, as long as you are not doing so to build up your own sense of importance. That will backfire. You don't want to compete with the prince. You want to influence the prince's thought processes and decision making only in ways that will redound to his or her benefit and that of the institution.

Not all presidents are perfect, of course, or hadn't you noticed? Presidential flaws may range from the occasional gaffe or inappropriate comment to the inability to listen to anything other than one's own voice to disingenuousness or worse. But what about the truly nasty president who nevertheless manages occasionally to rise to the top? One of the courtiers in Castiglione's book says that "we must pray God to grant us good masters for once we have them, we have to endure them as they are; because countless considerations force a gentleman not to leave a patron once he has begun to serve him: the misfortune lies in ever beginning; and in that case courtiers are like those unhappy birds that are born in some miserable valley" (p. 116). Another courtier advises that "if our courtier happens to find himself in the service of one who is wicked and malign, let him leave him as soon as he discovers this, that he may escape the great anguish that all good men feel in serving the wicked" (p. 116).

I have never had the experience of serving a malign prince, so I don't know for sure what I would do, but I think I would follow the latter courtier's advice and get out. Of course, most presidents are not truly evil, because it is difficult to get away with this in a context of shared governance. The presidents I would choose not to work with merely show signs of arrogance, incompetence, inconsiderateness, or blind ambition. Some are merely difficult and demanding.

One of the presidents I admire is Steve Trachtenburg, who has served as president of George Washington University for nineteen years. In fact, he had a wonderful piece in the most recent issue of *The Presidency*, an ACE publication, in which he speculates on the secrets of longevity for higher education presidents. His insights are wise and worthy of reflection, which is why I kept a copy of the article to pass on to one of my vice presidents and to keep for future reference. Before assuming the presidency, Trachtenburg was assistant to John Silber, the legendary president of Boston University. I can't think that it would have been an easy job, and yet to my knowledge Mr. Trachtenburg has never made any uncomplimentary comments about Mr. Silber, only that when he was ready to leave, he knew that he could be a good president.

As we further learn from Castiglione, the good courtier must be adept at protecting and guiding the prince: "It is certain that a man aims at the best end when he sees to it that his prince is deceived by no one, listens to no flatterers or slanderers or liars, and distinguishes good from evil, loving one and hating the other." Another courtier posits that sometimes "besides never hearing the truth about anything at all, princes are made drunk by the great license that rule gives; and by a profusion of delights are submerged in pleasures, and deceive themselves so and have their minds so corrupted—seeing themselves always obeyed and almost adored with so much reverence and praise, without ever the least contradiction, let alone censure—that from this ignorance they pass to an extreme self-conceit, so that then they become intolerant of any advice or opinion from others" (pp. 290–91).

Well, we wouldn't want that to happen, would we, so it is important to keep our princes humble. In the *Chronicle* article I referenced earlier, Steve Trachtenburg recounts a time when he was headed for a television interview. He donned a cap promoting the George Washington University women's basketball team, which was playing in the NCAA Final Four Championships. His assistant told him, "You look like a dork. Take off the hat." My executive assistant Cathie Bitz, who is here today, is a master at keeping me humble. The examples of her skill are far too numerous to recount here. Suffice it to say that when she sees me about ready to commit a blunder of some kind, she assumes this very quiet, reassuring voice and offers a few observations designed to make me see the error of my ways. Of course, sometimes she merely tells me to remove the spinach from my teeth.

When the courtiers are asked how they would respond to a prince seeking their advice on how to be effective, Signor Ottaviano replies that he would advise the prince to "choose from among his subjects a number of the noblest and wisest gentlemen, with whom to consult on everything, and that he should give them authority and free leave to speak their mind to him about all things without hesitation; and that he should act toward them in such a way as to show them all that he wished to know the truth in everything and that he detested all falsehood" (p. 315). As presidential assistants, you have a responsibility for ensuring—to the degree you can—that your president is advised by people whose motives and judgment can be trusted. You should help the president to hear what he or she needs to hear, not necessarily what he or she wants to hear. Through these efforts, says Signor Ottaviano, the courtier "will be able to realize that other part of his duty, which is not to allow his prince to be deceived, always to make known the truth about everything, and to set himself against flatterers and slanderers and all those who scheme to corrupt the mind of his prince in unworthy pleasures. . . . The office of a good courtier is to know the prince's nature and his inclinations . . . and then lead him to virtue" (pp. 330–32).

One person who understood these responsibilities well was Jim Scally, one of our founding members from the University of Kansas. At one point in our relationship he shared with me a memo he wrote at the request of Judith Ramaley, the incoming executive vice chancellor. She had asked Jim for his advice on selecting an assistant. Here is some of what Jim Scally had to say:

> Your use of an assistant will depend largely on your own administrative style, but some things will occur in spite of or in tandem with your style. Your assistant ought to be, with the secretarial staff, the office memory, keeper of traditions, controller of the files, etc. In that capacity she can save you from errors of either fact or style. She ought to be well connected—"networked" would be the term, I suppose—across campus, with her counterparts, key secretaries, deans and chairs, whomever might be a source of information, support, assistance to you. She should be able to brief you on upcoming meetings, individuals, the background of issues, with materials from the files where appropriate, and see that you are never surprised. She ought to be available when you need her, within reason. She should see as much as possible of the correspondence you receive, including confidential materials you believe it would be wise for her to know about. She is often likely to have information to supplement information you receive from others. Depending on your preference, she should ideally see all the mail first. . . . And a good assistant ought to be a stylistic chameleon, tailoring her writing style and vocabulary to yours. Within three months, your styles in official correspondence ought to be indistinguishable from one another.
>
> The more you involve your assistant in your work, the more efficient she can be as a true assistant: if she doesn't know the topic or content of a meeting, remember to brief her when you can. The inevitable follow-up then won't have to land only on your desk.
>
> I don't think people resent being referred to your assistant, so long as the assistant is one who gets along well with people—and so long as you don't give people the impression that your assistant is a lowlife of some kind. . . . Of

course there are some people who shouldn't ever be referred to an assistant, at least at first, but even many of them will welcome the information that your assistant has your trust and your ear, and is capable of assisting them.

A good assistant will probably argue with you from time to time, and a good executive will let her win when it's the right course. She won't argue for its own sake or to impose her own sense of "right." At least she shouldn't. She ought to be able to act as the devil's advocate on some issues (your choice), disagree openly when she really does, and have broad enough shoulders and enough patience to listen to you let off steam privately. She shouldn't need much stroking, but ought to get a lot of it anyway, but only when it is deserved. She shouldn't have to laugh at all your jokes, either.

It is not always good to take your assistant to meetings with you, but there are some where it is a very good idea indeed, and others where it will be essential. . . . She should be able to take care of many (most) of the walk-in visitors and much of the phone traffic as well, since the custom around here, on and off campus, is to call the highest possible office for the littlest matter.

Her job, in short, is to keep from you anything that keeps you from doing your job. A position like that of the executive vice chancellor can get to be like being nibbled to death by ducks. She is the one who ought to be able to prevent that. She ought to be good enough at what she does so that you are never fully aware of how much she in fact does.

If all this sounds like your assistant needs to be a paragon, consider the source. I'm one myself (assistant, not paragon).

Jim Scally is no longer with us, but his generosity of spirit, sharp wit, and excellent counsel live on. Though written twenty years ago, his advice on what to look for in an assistant is completely sound. And I hope you notice the resemblance between what Jim Scally had to say in this memo and Castiglione's advice of five hundred years ago. Some good counsel is timeless.

I can't end these reflections without noting that just as Castiglione's work is an excellent manual for the aspiring courtier or presidential assistant, the classic text for princely or presidential behavior might be said to be Machiavelli's *The Prince*. I mention that just so that you understand the depth and complexity of the challenge you face.

As someone who has served as a presidential assistant and who now benefits from the ministrations of a presidential assistant (two of them actually), I thoroughly appreciate the invaluable role that you play. As I'm sure you know, though you probably wouldn't say it out loud, we would truly be lost without you.

NOTE

1. Originally presented at the NAPAHE Annual Meeting, February 10, 2007. Used by permission.

REFERENCES

Castiglione, B. (1959). *The book of the courtier*. New York: Doubleday/Anchor Books.

Clemens, J. (1996–1997). Before you can lead. In *3.5 plus*. Jackson, MS: Phi Theta Kappa International Honor Society.

Montell, G. A. (2000, April 7). The president's alter ego. *Chronicle of Higher Education*.

APPENDIX B

ADDRESS DELIVERED TO THE SECOND ANNUAL MEETING OF THE NATIONAL ASSOCIATION OF PRESIDENTIAL ASSISTANTS IN HIGHER EDUCATION, JANUARY 18, 1989

James J. Scally[1]

As presidential assistants in higher education, we are something of an anomaly, standing somewhere between Cardinal Richelieu and the doorman, between H. R. Haldeman and Vanna White. There is the recurring, inevitable question, "What does the assistant to the president do?" I usually try a boyish grin, a shrug, and a discreet "I do what needs to be done." That's usually cool enough to deflect the conversation in other directions. Let them envision us hobnobbing with the mighty and powerful and talking on lofty intellectual planes, undisturbed by the trivia of ordinary existence. Let's look at a typical day and then talk about lofty planes!

Do they need to know, do we want them to know, about the endless paperwork, the telephone calls, the drop-in visitors, the complaints and the cranks, the leaking roof on the president's house, the stray dogs on campus, the showers that don't work or the chimes that do, the committee meetings, the protocol and menus, parking, the letters, speeches, and papers that have to be written (usually yesterday), the eternal committee meetings, and again the telephone calls? Would they care? Would they believe it? Would you?

You arrive at the office to learn that the computer is down for at least three hours—and you gave away all the typewriters two weeks ago. So that means the speech the boss needs for tomorrow can wait. Where to start? Try the phone messages: four parents, complaining; two trustees, no messages: so, problems, no doubt; a gaggle of reporters about some crisis or other; and four calls from people you've never heard of. One turns out to be an investment counselor who wants your money, one is a computer salesman who doesn't want to talk to Purchasing, and the other two are alums who don't much like anything that is going on and want to be sure you know it. Those answered, you graciously receive the angry faculty colleague who settled for you when he found out the president was out of town. Twenty precious minutes, but he leaves happy. He'll be back next week.

Tonight you have a guest speaker, A Great Man with highly controversial views. Dinner beforehand and reception afterward, a carefully selected guest list of VIPs, and a million details to check before then. You look over the meetings on your calendar and decide to skip two of them: the faculty executive committee and the commencement committee. Each meets for at least ninety minutes, and you can recite the agenda—and full details of the discussion—in your sleep. You call the two chairpersons and beg off, not knowing if they are happy or not that you won't be there.

The day's mail then hits your desk: two inches of junk mail, fourteen glossy reports from universities you didn't know existed, announcements of three interesting new books that you will never have time to read, invitations for the president to attend the ribbon-cutting at the new Stop-N-Shop and seventeen different dinners, most of them in towns too small to have a dining room, much less a restaurant, all of them with groups who are certain that he and he alone can make their program a success (which means a speech for each of them and guess who writes them all). The system is still down, but you don't have time to answer anything. It will all wait until tomorrow.

The president is back by now, so you stick your head in his office to assure him that everything is just fine for the evening program. He doesn't need to know that you have no idea where the speaker is, that you pray the great man will eventually show up for dinner, and that the students who volunteered to pick him up at the airport don't overturn the car or insult him. The boss then leaves, to be seen no more until dinner.

Lunch would be nice, but you settle for microwaving an envelope of what claims to be soup. No crackers. A diet soft drink: good for your waist, bad for your stomach. While you dine, you return some more phone calls, sorting through the mail while you are on the phone. They can't see you and they won't know you're reading unless you miss a question here and there. You spend the next hour or so entertaining a procession of vice presidents, deans, and office staff, each of whom has a problem they would prefer to see lying on your desk. You deflect a few, but most get what they want, which is your agreement to do part of their job, since the alternative is for no one to do it until the very last minute.

Then, after a day spent comforting the afflicted, placating the alumni, mediating between the vice presidents, writing out in longhand the speech you had hoped to postpone even longer, answering some of the mail, kow-towing to the random legislator or trustee, and seeing that the casualties receive decent burial, it's off to Alumni Hall to oversee final arrangements for that night's dinner and lecture. You just need a folder for your notes.

You open the supply cabinet, and the sky falls—literally. A three-pound glass fish, a gag gift the president's wife has sent to the office to get it out of her house, bounces off your head and slices open your hand. It seems like God's own judgment on you either for taking the job in the first place or for inviting that buffoon of a speaker. You put your hand to your head, so the blood runs down your face and onto your last clean white shirt, and the secretaries dial 911. They also take you into the restroom where one shoves your hand under cold water, another removes your glasses, another your tie, and you finally assert yourself when someone starts unbuttoning your shirt. The police arrive first, followed by reporters from the student paper and radio station, both of which monitor the police band and are salivating over the prospect that the president has somehow been injured. They are followed by the ambulance, which naturally brings a crowd to the front of the administration building.

You finally clear everyone out and get to the doctor's office to have your hand stitched, after explaining that no, you weren't bitten by a fish, but it's clearly all too complicated. You escape, stitched and bandaged, and go home to change, only to find that your other dark suit is at the cleaners. That's OK, since you haven't noticed the blood stains on your trousers, so you change your shirt and tie and go off to welcome the speaker, who insists on shaking hands and nearly brings you to your knees until he notices the bandages.

He's a nasty little brute who thinks he deserves better quality liquor—which he doesn't—and reminds you that he drew a crowd of 7,000 at Si-wash State—which has an enrollment of only 1,500. You think he'll be lucky to hold on to the dinner guests, but you manage to dance around that one without answering. You escape by introducing him to the nearest person, who turns out to be a student politician who distributed condoms at enroll-ment as a consciousness-raising maneuver. By then your hand is throbbing because you keep forgetting not to shake hands, but you eventually get everyone seated and dinner is served.

You don't eat dinner, of course, because the police ask you to step outside and discuss plans for handling the demonstrators who have now filled the first eighteen rows in the hall, including the seats reserved for the family that endowed the lecture series and the other dinner guests.

You get back just in time to watch the dessert plates disappear into the kitchen, and you move everyone off to the auditorium. You have persuaded the protesters to move back a bit, and you get everyone seated, only to find that: (a) the sound system isn't working, (b) the technician has gone home for dinner, and (c) in your absence the guest of honor obviously reversed his opinion about the quality of your gin. You turn him loose anyway, having fixed the speakers with the help of a friendly cop, and you watch in fascination a forty-five-minute performance that stuns even the protesters into silence. The great man then lurches off stage to a very mixed reaction, and it's off to the reception where he takes a fancy to the teetotaling wife of your board chairman. You pry them apart as her husband murmurs something about calling you tomorrow, and you deposit the star of the evening behind a large fern in time to go outside and deal with the protesters who are asserting their right to join the party.

You are tempted to let them in, but you review the guest list and decide that the big cigars inside aren't quite ready for this particular slice of campus life. You are hypnotized by the ensuing half-hour discussion of the philosophical bases of free expression and the minutiae of the Constitution, and the events of the day finally catch up with you. In front of the reporters and cameras you announce that the protesters may parade back and forth until the cows come home, but you'll see them all fry in hell before you let them step one foot inside the door.

With that, you haul Wee Willie Winkie out of the reception and pour him into the motel, conscious every minute that you are the one who has to drive him to the airport the next morning at five. You get home in time for the midnight news. The protesters look innocent as newborns and you look—and sound—like something out of the Brothers Grimm. Your wife tells you there have been six calls from reporters, two from the president, and one, just one, from the chairman of the board. And right before you fall asleep, a vision appears: Scarlett O'Hara, chin up and eyes shining, reminding you that "tomorrow is another day."

And people wonder why we love our work!

In thinking about our meeting, I have been haunted by an aphorism from Hillel, the great Talmudist and teacher who lived two millennia ago. "If I am not for myself," he asked, "who will be for me? And if I am not for others, what am I?" It is a paradox worth considering in those rare moments when we reflect on our work: "If I am not for myself, who will be for me? And if I am not for others, what am I?" It is both an inquiry and a prescription. Naturally, we are for ourselves. We choose a career that we hope will bring rewards of a deeply satisfying kind. Those of us who have taken on the duties of assistant to a president or chancellor share at least one trait: a willingness to serve, to accept both the limitations and the opportunities implicit in the designation "assistant." There is a fulfillment in service, whether as a temporary pursuit or as a lifelong commitment. Those who cannot understand our choice find their fulfillment elsewhere. Neither we nor they are lessened by the choice. It is simply a matter of temperament.

We serve individual presidents or chancellors or an institution. We serve higher education. Not that we are altruists, sacrificing ourselves on the altar of higher education or for the good of ol' Woebegone State. We are human, and we look out for ourselves. But if we find satisfaction in the work we do, if we find it professionally valid and rewarding, it is most likely because we do more than just look out for ourselves.

We are defined professionally in part by our bosses, their styles, needs, and preferences; by the characteristics of our institutions; and by what we do and how we do it. But we are more fully defined by the personal dimensions we bring to our work. And the most important of those personal traits must surely be our willingness to look beyond self-interests to the broader needs and concerns of the individuals and institutions we serve.

I suspect the number of college and university presidents who read Hillel is quite small. But I believe that virtually all of them would read his paradoxical questions with a shock of recognition, and might think of us. And with a little prompting, each of those presidents would admit that what he or she wants in an assistant is someone intelligent, hardworking, and talented. But what each president hopes for is someone wise enough to at least consider those questions as valid guideposts. I believe we do that, and that as presidential assistants in higher education we should be proud of the part we play in our great common endeavor.

Just last week, I received a call from someone interested in becoming a presidential assistant. He asked, hopefully, if there was somewhere to go for preparation. I said "San Diego" [site of the ACE/NAPAHE meeting—ed.], of course, but then told him I knew of no training or preparation he might pursue.

What I might have said was, look first into yourself. Honestly consider whether you wish to lend yourself to another, or commit yourself wholly to an institution you love and respect. Ask yourself, can you be fulfilled by standing in someone else's shadow—someone whose faults and failings you may come to know as well as you know your own—and not be diminished? Are you willing to take on a professional life best characterized by its loneliness, since much of what you will do can never be shared with anyone else? Are you able—and willing—to speak always for another without compromising either him or yourself? Can you consider the paradox of Rabbi Hillel I quoted earlier, consider it with humility, equanimity, and with the hope of someday understanding it fully?

If you can answer yes to these questions, and can do so with honesty, eagerness, and a happy heart, then, my friends, I welcome you to a most rewarding professional life, and to a uniquely satisfying company of fellow spirits, the National Association of Presidential Assistants in Higher Education.

NOTE

1. Previously published in the *NAPAHE News*, 4(1–2, October 1997). Used by permission.

ABOUT THE CONTRIBUTORS

Kevin Boatright is director of communications in the Office of Research and Graduate Studies at the University of Kansas (KU). He came to KU in 2002 as senior deputy to the executive vice chancellor for external affairs. This followed ten years in university relations with the University of Wisconsin (UW) System administration in Madison, where he rose to the position of assistant vice president. Principal duties in these positions encompassed strategic communications, news media relations, government relations, and special projects. He previously served in editorial and public affairs positions with UW–Platteville, the University of Northern Iowa, and the Fisher Controls division of Monsanto. In all of these roles he has worked with senior-level leadership on executive communications, including speechwriting for university presidents and chancellors. He holds master's degrees from UW–Madison (higher education administration), Northern Iowa (history), and the University of Iowa (journalism), with a bachelor's degree in English from Nebraska Wesleyan University.

John Cummins spent his entire career (1972–2008) in higher education administration at the University of California, Berkeley. He worked for five chancellors over that period of time in a variety of capacities including managing federal, state, and local governmental relations; internal audits; whistleblower investigations; media relations and public affairs; intercollegiate athletics; and campus crises. He was a senior advisor and chief of staff to four chancellors. He also worked at the Institute of Governmental Studies at Berkeley, where he founded the California Policy Research Center, a joint public policy research enterprise between the University of California and the state government. He received his Ph.D. in education from the University of Wisconsin–Milwaukee, and his bachelor's degree in philosophy and theology from Marquette University.

Mark P. Curchack is the executive director of the president's office, the associate vice president for planning and assessment, and the secretary to the board at Arcadia University in Glenside, Pennsylvania. He returned to a role in the president's office after serving five years as graduate dean at Arcadia, and, before that, fifteen years as executive assistant to the president. He has been active in NAPAHE since its inception in 1988, serving twice as the program chair, and twice as chair of the board. In 2003 he received the organization's first Distinguished Service Award. He has also been active in the SCUP (Society for College and University Planning), and in 2009 was elected chair of the mid-Atlantic region. Mark has taught anthropology at Arcadia, and, prior to that, at Western Michigan University. His Ph.D. in anthropology is from the University of California, Berkeley. He holds a bachelor's degree from Yale University, and has attended the Harvard Graduate School of Education Management Development Program.

Antoinette G. Gifford has been the director of institutional research and special projects at Bank Street College since 2007. Prior to that she served as special assistant to the president and chief of staff at Bank Street College from 1995 to 2007. Her responsibilities included oversight of the president's office, serving as the assistant secretary to the board of trustees, strategic planning, and coordination of the leadership team. She served as a member of the board of NAPAHE for six years, including three years chairing the membership committee. A policy researcher by training, she received her undergraduate degree from Swarthmore College and her master's degree in public policy from the University of California, Berkeley. She is currently a doctoral student at New York University.

Steven J. Givens is associate vice chancellor and executive director of university communications at Washington University in St. Louis, where he is responsible for the planning and implementation of public affairs strategies and programs for local, national, and international news initiatives as well as issues management. Prior to being named to this position in January 2007, he served for nine years as assistant to Chancellor Mark S. Wrighton, during which time he led the steering committees for two presidential debates. He was a member of NAPAHE from 1998 until 2006 and served as a board member during 2005–2006. He holds a bachelor's degree in English literature and a master's degree in education, both from the University of Missouri, St. Louis.

Richard P. Haven is the interim dean of the College of Arts and Communication and a professor of communication at the University of Wisconsin–Whitewater. At UW–Whitewater he has also worked as the assistant to the chancellor, chair of the faculty senate, chair of the communication department, and associate dean of the College of Arts and Communication. Dr. Haven has served as the speechwriter for four chancellors over a fifteen-year period. He received his bachelor's and master's degrees from Ball State University and his Ph.D. from the University of Wisconsin–Madison. Dr. Haven has taught public speaking, persuasion, speechwriting, and American public address. He is a regular guest expert on Wisconsin Public Radio as well as several commercial radio stations in southeastern Wisconsin. Dr. Haven also helped identify the 100 Greatest American Speeches of the Twentieth Century. An active member of NAPAHE for many years, he has presented numerous workshops on executive speechwriting at the annual NAPAHE national conference, in conjunction with his fellow author, Kevin Boatright.

Laura Katrenicz has served as executive assistant to the president at Luzerne County Community College since 1995. She teaches English composition and business English as a part-time instructor. Laura is a graduate of Leadership Wilkes-Barre and the National Institute of Leadership Development (NILD), and has been an active member of NAPAHE. She received her master's degree in communications from Marywood University and her bachelor's degree from Pennsylvania State University.

Nancy Kelly was secretary of the college and senior advisor to the president at Hampshire College in Amherst, Massachusetts, until 2009, where she also oversaw college communications. She has served as administrator or faculty at the University of Massachusetts, Boston; Salem State College; and Northern Essex Community College; and has collaborated with former Hampshire College president Gregory S. Prince Jr. on numerous journal articles and book chapters on a variety of topics related to higher education. Nancy holds a B.A. summa cum laude from the University of Massachusetts, Boston, and an M.A. from Claremont Graduate University.

Marcus Lingenfelter is the vice president for advancement at Harrisburg University of Science and Technology. He is responsible for development, government affairs, communications and marketing, and alumni and constituent relations. Prior to working at Harrisburg University, Marcus served as senior education program coordinator at the Council for Advancement and Support of Education; the inaugural Allan and Roberta Ostar Administrative Fellow and Graduate Teaching Assistant at the Pennsylvania State University; associate director of development for the Curry School of Education at the University of Virginia; and executive assistant to the president, director of government affairs, and assistant vice president for government, corporate, and foundation relations at Widener University. Marcus earned a B.S. from East Stroudsburg University and an M.Ed. in higher education from the Pennsylvania State University. He attended Harvard University's Institute for Educational Management, and is presently completing a Ph.D. in higher education from Penn State.

Michael R. McGreevey is the vice president for development at Wells College. Previous to this appointment, he served as the senior advisor to the president at Ithaca College for nearly ten years. Other positions he has held during his twenty-year tenure at Ithaca College include director for special programs (Institutional Advancement), interim director for alumni relations, director of the London Center, special assistant for enrollment planning, and assistant director for campus activities and orientation. He holds a B.A. in communications from Bowling Green State University, an M.Ed. in higher education administration from the University of Vermont, and an M.S. in communications from Ithaca College. In addition, he has participated in intensive professional development programs including the Harvard School of Education's Management Development Program, The Center for Creative Leadership's Management Development Program, and the Council for the Advancement of Education's (CASE) summer institute. He has been active with the NAPAHE over the years as a member and chair of the board of directors and served as the NAPAHE 2004 annual meeting and conference chair.

Belinda Miles is president of Cuyahoga Community College's Eastern Campus in Cleveland, Ohio. She previously served the college as dean of academic affairs and in other dean roles. Other prior positions include faculty and administrative posts at LaGuardia Community College, Nassau Community College, University of Akron, and Columbia University. She serves as a member of the International President's Advisory Board for the

Chair Academy, as a career advisor for the Higher Education Resource Services Summer Institute for Women in Higher Education Administration, and as a member of the board of directors for various Cleveland-area community organizations. Dr. Miles earned an M.A. in educational psychology and an Ed.D. in higher education organization and leadership development from Columbia University. Her B.A. in political science is from the City University of New York at York College.

Anthony R. Ross is vice president for student affairs and associate professor in the Charter College of Education at California State University, Los Angeles (CSULA). He joined CSULA in July 2000. Prior to joining CSULA, he served as vice president for development with Edison Learning in 1999. From 1994 to 1999, Dr. Ross served as associate to the president and later, interim vice president for student affairs at Wichita State University. During his tenure as associate to the president, he was a member of the board of directors of NAPAHE from 1995 to 1999, and was named chair of the association in 1997. Prior to his arrival at Wichita State, Dr. Ross served Northern Arizona University in such key roles as assistant vice president for student services, dean of students, associate dean of students, and assistant dean of students from 1983 to 1994. He served as director of the Higher Education Opportunity Program at St. Lawrence University from 1976 to 1981. He began his career at Utica College in 1975 as a counselor in the Higher Education Opportunity Program. He earned his bachelor's degree in sociology and his master's degree in counseling from St. Lawrence University, and his doctorate in educational administration and leadership from Northern Arizona University. His leadership training includes the Harvard Graduate School of Education Institute for Educational Management in addition to the NASPA Richard Stevens Institute for Leadership.

James J. Scally was one of the founders of the National Association of Presidential Assistants in Higher Education. From 1976 to 1995 he served as the assistant to four chancellors of the University of Kansas (KU). His talks at the first several meetings of NAPAHE were often the highlight of a meeting. An English scholar, he was president of the Lawrence Lyric Opera. In 1995 he became the assistant dean of the School of Fine Arts at KU, a position he held at the time of his death a year later.

Marc Schaeffer currently serves as chief of staff to the president and board of trustees at William Paterson University in Wayne, New Jersey, where he began working for the president in 1994 as executive assistant. He oversees all operational functions of the president's office and serves as a policy advisor to the board and president and a member of his cabinet. He authors, in consultation with the board chair and committee chairs, all trustee meeting and committee agendas, committee minutes, and trustee correspondence. Prior to working for the president, he served as assistant vice president for academic affairs responsible for managing the academic budget, space allocation, academic affairs personnel, and course data management and academic computing. Dr. Schaeffer serves on the board of NAPAHE, and is the incoming chair of the AGB Board Professionals marketing and membership committee and a member of its leadership group. Dr. Schaeffer earned an Ed.D. in higher education from Columbia University–Teachers College in 1991, a master's in college counseling and student development from Hunter College of CUNY in 1976, and a bachelor's degree, cum laude, in psychology from Queens College of CUNY in 1974.

Elizabeth Wright Schoenfeld is the executive assistant to the president at Western Washington University in Bellingham, Washington. Before coming to Western, she served as special assistant to the chancellor at the University of Wisconsin Colleges, as interim dean of UW–Rock County, and as executive assistant to the executive vice president of the University of Wisconsin System. She has been a member of NAPAHE since its first meeting in 1988, serving as a member of the board from 1997 to 2005, as the program chair in 2000, and as chair of the board in 2000–2001. In 2006, she received the organization's Distinguished Service Award. Her J.D., M.P.A., and M.A. in political science are from the University of Wisconsin–Madison, and she has attended the Harvard Graduate School of Education Institute for Management Education. She holds a bachelor's degree from the University of Wisconsin–Milwaukee.

Emily Sinsabaugh has served since February 2007 as the vice president for university relations at St. Bonaventure University located near Olean, New York. She is responsible for marketing, communications, fund-raising, and alumni relations. She previously served for nearly twelve years as the executive to the president at Edinboro University of Pennsylvania. Among her varied responsibilities were policy development, university communications, public relations, and special events. She was elected chair of NAPAHE and also served as a member of the NAPAHE board of directors for eight years. Emily earned both her bachelor's and master's degrees in communication from Edinboro University of Pennsylvania and a Ph.D. in higher education from the State University of New York at Buffalo.

Stephen Joel Trachtenberg is president emeritus and University Professor of Public Service at The George Washington University. He served as GW's fifteenth president for nearly two decades, from 1988 to 2007. Trachtenberg came to GW from the University of Hartford, where he had been president for eleven years. He also held positions as vice president for academic services and academic dean of the College of Liberal Arts at Boston University, and served as the special assistant to the U.S. Education Commissioner, Department of Health, Education, and Welfare. Trachtenberg is a member of the Council on Foreign Relations, Phi Beta Kappa, and the boards of directors of the Chiang Chen Industrial Charity Foundation in Hong Kong, the Bankinter Foundation in Madrid, and the Ditchley Foundation in England. He is a fellow of the American Academy of Arts and Sciences and a fellow of the National Academy of Public Administration. Trachtenberg chairs the Rhodes Scholarships Selection Committee for Maryland and the District of Columbia. He has published five books and is coeditor of two. Trachtenberg has served on numerous boards including the Chamber of Commerce, the Board of Trade, the Federal City Council, the Loctite Corporation, and MNC and Riggs Banks. Trachtenberg earned a B.A. from Columbia University, a J.D. from Yale University, and a master's of public administration from Harvard University. In addition, he holds sixteen honorary doctoral degrees, including a doctor of laws from his alma mater, Columbia University.

Pamela Transue has served as president of Tacoma Community College (TCC) since 1997. Dr. Transue is active in local civic improvement efforts and in regional and national professional activities. She served as chair of the board of the American Association of Community Colleges, as secretary of the board of the American Council on Education, and as president of COMBASE, a national organization devoted to community-based learning. She is president-elect of the Washington Association of Community and Technical Colleges, and she serves on a number of community boards. Dr. Transue was educated at the University of Washington, where she earned her bachelor's degree; the Ohio State University, where she earned her master's and Ph.D.; and Harvard, where she completed the Institute of Educational Management. She is the author of two books and numerous articles. Before coming to TCC, she served as executive dean at Portland Community College and as special assistant to the president at the University of Washington. Dr. Transue is an active Rotarian and a Paul Harris Fellow.